# FOR SUCH A TIME AS THIS

## Vonette Z. Bright

Fleming H. Revell Company
Old Tappan, New Jersey

Library of Congress Cataloging in Publication Data

Bright, Vonette Z.
    For such a time as this.
      1.  Women—Religious life.  2.  Christian life—
1960-      3.  Bright, Vonette Z.  I.  Title.
BV4527.B72      248'.843      76-25176
ISBN 0-8007-0831-8

With gratitude to my parents, Roy and Margaret Zachary, who invested their lives in their four children. Their sacrifice to provide the best that they could offer—as well as their example, encouragement, and love—has largely prepared me for God's call "for such a time as this."

# Contents

# Foreword

*Dear Vonette,*

Two weeks ago, my secretary told me you desired a foreword from me for your book: *For Such a Time as This.* I had just returned from a witnessing and singing engagement for a Sunday church rally at the Calgary Stampede in Alberta, Canada and was on my way to Orlando, Florida for another engagement. She said she emphatically informed you: "No way, *no way*—could Dale do this; it is impossible with her schedule." I agreed with her response.

Then my eyes fell upon your manuscript title: *For Such a Time as This,* and immediately there flashed into my mind a picture of our late and beloved teacher, Miss Henrietta Mears, as I remember her at a Forest Home Retreat here in California during the flourishing days of the Hollywood Christian Group.

Miss Mears, batting those clear, direct eyes at us, once declared: "Who knows what the Lord has for us for such a time as this?" Then she told the beautiful story of Queen Esther who was willing to be used of the Lord to save His people—even at the risk of her own life.

Another picture flashed: the "Moorish Castle" at Bel Air, when you and your fine husband, Bill, along with Miss Mears, shared that castle for God.

Then came a picture of me witnessing one Sunday evening at a church at the UCLA Campus to some young students when Campus Crusade for Christ was just beginning . . . .

I tucked your manuscript under my arm, and brought it home, placing it at my bedside where I keep inspirational reading, along with my Bible, to prepare me for sleep.

Vonette, last night I started to read *For Such a Time as This* and was overwhelmed at what "the Lord hath done" through you. Indeed, He has used you in this book to reach women everywhere for just *such times* as *these,* when women need to understand that God, in Christ, in His Holy Spirit, is calling women to become *His* Holy Women—to be strategically used in more ways than a mere *foreword* can possibly delineate.

I cannot remember reading a more honest, clearly instructional, obviously God-inspired book for women in my entire life. Incidentally, men could use it, too! In many ways, Vonette, you and I are quite alike in both temperament and drive, with an innate desire for complete honesty in our Christianity.

Women everywhere! Give yourselves a break and read this book! If you are *not* Christians, you need it. If you *are* Christians, you need it. I myself, needed very much to read this book *for such a time as this* in my own life and Christian walk.

In my humble opinion, *For Such a Time as This* is a masterpiece. Our Risen Christ, I believe, directed the writing of it for women. He, truly, is *Women's Liberation* in the highest sense of the term, for it was He who really began women's *liberation.* He has been *liberating* us ever since. This I know, for He *liberated* me.

God speed you and your message, Vonette!

*In Christian love and esteem,*

DALE EVANS ROGERS

# Introduction

Ten years ago when a publisher first asked me to write a book, I was excited and flattered. But each year after that invitation, I found my responsibilities to my family, home, and ministry so time-consuming that it was easy to procrastinate. Yet, the Lord has kept the desire burning in my heart to write about the practical, workable answers I have found in the Christian life. Even though this has been the busiest year of my life, with the production of two prayer manuals and the expansion of the prayer workshops for the Great Commission Prayer Crusade, it has seemed to me that this book should be published this year or never.

Most upon my heart is the desire to see women find answers to their daily problems and to become God's maximum women and, like Esther of old, to make their lives count for Christ for just such a time as this. My prayer is that this book will help all readers to think creatively about their accountability to God and to be inspired to greater commitment and more effective action.

The Old Testament records the remarkable story of a beautiful queen named Esther, wife of King Ahasuerus. She was a Jew as was her uncle, Mordecai, who had found favor with the king in his court. Haman was a man of great authority and considerable influence with the king who sent out an order that all of the Jews were to be killed. Queen Esther was challenged by her uncle to intercede before the king in behalf of her fellow Jews. To do so was to risk her life should the king not look with favor upon her and her request. Mordecai reminded her that without her help her people would perish, and she would perish with them. He concluded his plea for her intercession before the king in behalf of the Jews with these prophetic words: "Who knows but what you have come to the King for such a time as this?" At the risk of her life she stood before the king to plead for her people. The plea was heard and granted. God gave her favor with the king and her people were spared.

Women of today are faced with a similar challenge. Many of the world's leaders believe civilization is facing its darkest hour and if freedom is to survive, women must play an important role in preserving that freedom.

Doctor Charles Malik, former president of the United Nations General Assembly and professor of American University of Beirut, Lebanon, in private conversation a few months ago said, "The fastest way to see the world changed is to organize the women of the world."

Oh, dear women, let us unite in building a better world. Let us begin to look at life from God's viewpoint and consider what He might have us do.

# Acknowledgments

This is an "our" book. I have come to the conclusion that all books, and particularly those of busy people, are "our" books. Without the prodding of Bill Barbour and the encouragement from Ernie Owen of Fleming H. Revell, I would never have started.

Then an angel in the form of Carol Barrington, a Campus Crusade for Christ staff member, descended into my path. Without the commitment of her time as she taped hour after hour of conversation, edited transcribed tapes and brought me the results for additions, corrections, and rewriting, this manuscript could never have been completed in the time limit. I am forever indebted to her and to her husband, Jay, who shared his wife's time with me.

I am grateful to Lawson and Fran Ridgeway for providing an ideal place to retreat for rest, meditation, and writing.

Janet Kobobel, Jan Roemer, Judy Douglass, and Erma Griswald added their valuable suggestions. Miriam Watne, Lynn Hedstrand, and others transcribed tapes and typed rough and final copy.

The Great Commission Prayer Crusade staff shared my divided attention. Louise Jennings, my personal secretary for five years, and now Brenda Tate in that position, ably assisted me. Carolee Nutt, my assistant in household management and entertaining, did everything possible to free my time.

My two dear sons, Zac and Brad, patiently endured an involved mother and enthusiastically cooperated and encouraged me to travel and speak so that I could pass the things I had learned and experienced on to others. Now that they are away at school, I have had more time to put these truths in writing.

Most of all, I thank my precious husband, who pushed me into a leadership position, sharing generously the opportunities of ministry, and has been a Christian example in living everything he professes. His confidence in me, his encouragement, his love, his protective concern, and his availability, along with his determination that I be "my own person have provided real inspiration and motivation as I seek to be God's maximum woman for just such a time as this.

# FOR SUCH A
# TIME AS THIS

# 1 Not Enough to Last a Lifetime

If material things can bring happiness, I should have been one of the happiest young women in the world. I had almost everything any woman could ask for, from all outward appearances: a handsome, successful husband; a beautiful and elegantly furnished home in famous Bel Air, California, which is one of the most exclusive areas in the world; domestic help; and many loving friends. The plans and dreams which my businessman husband, Bill Bright, and I had shared during our engagement now seemed to be realized. What else could one ask for? In spite of all I had to enjoy—success, prestige, and material blessings—there was still the dissatisfaction, emptiness, and frustration that countless women in all stations of life experience.

My dreaming had begun in the small town of Coweta, Oklahoma, where Bill and I attended high school. Bill was five years older than I, and was one of the most outstanding young men in our town. As we were growing up, I watched him closely and with special interest, but because of our age difference, never with a romantic interest.

During the summer after my freshman year at Texas Woman's University, I unexpectedly received a letter from William R. Bright, president of Bright's California Confections, which marketed its fancy foods—fruits, candies, jam and jellies, and other epicurean delights—through exclusive shops and the major department stores in the United States and Canada.

I was thrilled to receive the letter and could hardly wait to tell my father I had heard from William. After listening to my report, he commented, "Well, our hometown boy has gone away and made good, and now he's going to come home for his bride."

Because of embarrassment and pride, I decided William Bright would never know how thrilled I was to receive his letter, but "never" was to last for five and a half months. Summer soon became fall, and I left for school with my letter discreetly tucked among my keepsakes. One evening, while cleaning out my desk drawers, I came across the letter. After an animated conversation with my roommate on the qualities of Bill Bright, I spent the rest of the evening writing a ten-page "note," undaunted by the fact that I had not seen him in two and a half years.

The airmail, special-delivery reply I received was as exciting as his request to telephone me. Because it was during the war, long-distance telephone conversations had to be made by appointment. So I wrote back suggesting an appropriate time.

During this time a movie talent scout from Hollywood was on our campus, and everyone was talking about who would be invited for a screen test. When the telephone call came from Hollywood, where Bill's business was located, the housemother allowed it to be placed personally to me in her apartment. In her excitement she searched each floor of the dormitory, calling out again and again, "Vonette Zachary." Breathless but determined, she found me on the fourth floor, and enthusiastically announced that I had a call from Hollywood. With all the commotion, girls from every floor were standing in the hall eagerly awaiting the results of my call. My heart sang with excitement to hear from Bill, but no one was more disappointed than our housemother to learn that my call was from just a young suitor in California.

Correspondence between Bill and me began to flourish, and before long we were writing daily. Since Bill was well established in business, he could afford to be more attentive than most college girls' boyfriends. Every week I received flowers, candy, a telegram or a telephone call, and it was not long before Bill was known on campus as the "Candy Man."

He arrived on campus during March for his first visit. After a delightful dinner, we found a quiet spot and talked of what had happened in the intervening years since we had seen each other. During the course of our conversation, Bill proposed marriage. We sometimes jokingly argue about whether I said yes that first night or later, but I'm certain I gave him enough encouragement that he was sure of a positive answer.

Almost three years passed before Bill and I were married. During our long engagement many significant events took place in our lives. First, some changes occurred in Bill's life which were disturbing to me. He had been attending Hollywood Presbyterian Church in California, and through the influence of Dr. Louis Evans, Sr., and Dr. Henrietta Mears, had dedicated his life to Christ.

That in itself was fine; it was alarming to me, however, to see the sincerity and totality of his commitment. He was sending me in his letters passages of Scripture to read; but they did not mean the same thing to me as they did to him. He would ask me to pray about certain things, yet I knew that one must be far more devout than I was to pray and receive answers. I began to realize that I was engaged to a man to whom Christ meant everything in his life, while Christ was not real to me.

Desperately feeling the need to correct Bill's position and save our future marriage, I planned a trip to California. Upon leaving, I promised my college roommate that I would come back without a ring unless my fiancé changed what I considered his extreme religious views and gave up his fanaticism.

Soon after arriving in California, I met many of the people with whom Bill had become involved at Hollywood Presbyterian Church. As I watched and listened to them talk about "what God had done in my life," or "what God showed me in my personal Bible study today," I kept thinking to myself, *This is the sharpest bunch of kooks I've ever seen.* I would ask them how they knew God had answered their prayers, or how they knew God showed them verses from the Bible. But I especially wanted to know how they knew God as personally as they seemed to. They would explain that their assurance was based on a personal relationship with Jesus Christ.

One evening as Bill and I were discussing what had taken place in his life and in the lives of his friends, I felt pretty sure their excitement would soon pass. Their faith was just new to them.

I also realized that Bill's faith was right for him, but I had tried it, and it hadn't worked for me. I came from a church background and had attended church functions all my life, and I knew it did not hold for me what Jesus Christ held for Bill and his friends.

In no way did I want to stand in the way of Bill's relationship with God, so I came to the conclusion that perhaps the best thing to do was simply bow out of his life even though I loved him dearly. I decided to wait until the end of the week, return his ring, and then we would go our separate ways.

Bill suggested that perhaps I would like to talk with Dr. Henrietta Mears, director of Christian education at Bill's church and, in my opinion, one of the great women of our time. After a long period of discussion with her, she helped me realize who Jesus Christ is and why He came to this world. Much to Bill Bright's delight and relief, and to my surprise, I made my commitment to Jesus Christ, a commitment which I thought I had made as a little girl but one which had long since lost its meaning and relevance in my life.

As the week with Bill came to a close, I left with an exciting relationship with Jesus Christ, a shiny diamond ring, and a wedding date set for December 30, 1948.

In the first months after our wedding, we enjoyed a great deal of time together. Unfortunately, this was not to last for long. We were extremely happy but, as Bill's responsibilities increased, our time together decreased. In addition to his usual busy schedule, Bill fervently desired to learn more about his Christian faith. Before our marriage he had attended Princeton Theological Seminary, but business responsibilities forced him to return to California. In the meantime Fuller Theological Seminary had opened in Pasadena, and now he could continue his business interests while enrolled in seminary. He managed his responsibilities well, while I became involved in totally unrelated activities.

After we settled in our home, I had very little to fill my time. Once I had made breakfast, seen Bill off to the office or to seminary, and straightened the house, I had to look for things to do. I found I was washing windows, painting woodwork, doing things which did not have to be done but filled up time.

My neighbor, Miss Emmeline Pankhurst, had been very active in the woman-suffrage movement in England. It was her opinion that, because of my training and education, I was far too intelligent to spend time washing windows, sweeping patios, and doing things which did not have to be done. She bluntly told me that my successful husband should pay to have these things done so that I could spend my time on more challenging and profitable pursuits.

I chuckled at her advice for I was thrilled to have my own home and to be Bill Bright's wife, but at the same time, I found myself going the long way about doing tasks because I wanted to keep busy until Bill got home. Many times I walked from our little house at the top of a hill above Hollywood Boulevard down to a store on the boulevard and back, about a three-mile distance, in order to fill the hours.

As the months passed and Miss Pankhurst continued to instruct me in the ills of housewifery, it began to make an impression. I soon began to question whether or not being domestically involved was really satisfying. As a young girl, I had done enough domestic tasks at home to realize there was not fulfillment for a lifetime in just doing housework.

Bill did not like the idea of my working outside the home, but I asked him to allow me to have the opportunity to put my teaching abilities and years of training into practice. I thought it would be the one time in my life when I could prove the practicality of my many years in school. Bill finally agreed, and I received an offer to teach in the Los Angeles school system.

Teaching was exciting to me. I loved the children and enjoyed investing my life in the lives of my students. I enrolled in graduate school to enhance my abilities. I even had the thrill of developing a course of study that was taught for the first time in the Los Angeles city school system.

In February 1951, as my teaching career was developing and Bill was in the final weeks of seminary, God gave him the vision for Campus Crusade for Christ, an organization designed to take the claims of Christ to college students and ultimately to the entire world. He was excited that God had revealed what He wanted him to do.

On the other hand, I was very apprehensive, though I was careful not to let Bill know my fears or to deflate his dream. In my mind's eye I could see everything we had talked about, dreamed of, and hoped for, fading into oblivion. Both of us had very expensive appetites, and material possessions meant a great deal to us. Now Bill talked about selling our business, moving to the UCLA campus, and living by faith. But I didn't know anybody who lived by faith in the fashion that I wanted to live.

I began to think of alternatives to Bill's plan. Secretly I hoped we couldn't sell the business and felt we could test whether or not the vision for Campus Crusade for Christ was from God by asking an exorbitant price for the business.

After discussing it with Bill, he let me set the price. Much to my surprise, the first caller, a man very familiar with the business, bought it. There was no human explanation for its sale, either for the amount for which it was sold or for the speed with which it was sold. Surely this was a confirmation from the Lord that He was leading us to start the ministry with students. On October 1, 1951, we moved to a home only a few blocks from the UCLA campus.

Suddenly our life changed course. I was juggling my teaching and my classes in graduate school with my domestic responsibilities, fitting into Bill's plans, entertaining, and being involved with the ministry. Bill was very helpful during this time. Many times I would come home from teaching to find dinner prepared and an evening meeting scheduled to talk to the many students who were interested in knowing about Jesus Christ. It was exciting but also tiring and sometimes confusing.

Bill's enthusiasm was contagious, and I was pleased that he was having such an exciting ministry, but I was also involved and having an interesting opportunity to express myself as a teacher. I was eager to tell him about what had happened in the classroom or in my relationships with some of the other teachers, or the opportunities I had been given for advancement. Bill was always interested and very complimentary, but there was little that I was doing that was as exciting as his involvement in winning and discipling others for Christ. It was obvious that we were both too busy to really communicate. As yet there were no marital difficulties, but I realized that if we proceeded in this manner for long, I would develop a profession completely apart from my husband, and Bill's ministry would grow without me. Since neither one of us wanted this type of marriage relationship, I began to look for ways to become involved with him.

As the months passed, Bill became increasingly busy with the students on the UCLA campus. He needed help, especially a woman to work with the coeds. I knew this person would be working very closely with my husband, sharing his dream. Though I had never been trained to help others in their Christian faith, I wanted to be his partner. I felt if I were given enough time to study, to mature, to really apply Christ's principles in my life, I could qualify as that woman to work with the girls. Bill was pleased, so I resigned from my teaching position to help him.

It was exciting to be involved in his ministry, and for the first time I felt I was in a place marked just for me. I was happy to have time for Bible study and to be able to learn so much from God's Word. I was pleased to have the privilege of working with students. It seemed that all I had to do was make an appointment to talk about the claims of Jesus Christ and how He could be real in a person's life, and that individual would respond. During the first semester I saw at least fifty young women receive Jesus Christ as their Savior. I was spending from six to eight hours every day counseling with students on campus, introducing girls to Christ, and helping them grow in their new faith. On Tuesday evenings, tens, sometimes hundreds of students met in various fraternities, sororities, or in our home for evangelistic meetings, which we now call College Life. Then on Saturday mornings many students came to our home for discipleship meetings, prayer, and Bible study.

It was exciting to see so many students respond to the training they received at our home. Consequently it didn't bother me to do housework at inconvenient times. Very often I would do my domestic tasks very late at night, or I would dash home from campus to do a load of laundry or prepare dinner. At this time we had four of the Campus Crusade for Christ staff members living with us, sometimes a few more, so we seldom had less than six for dinner. Although the staff members were very helpful, there was always plenty of work to do.

By the summer of 1953, the ministry was firmly established and hundreds of students were becoming involved. Though Bill still had some responsibility in business, the ministry demanded most of our time. Most of the meetings were held in fraternity and sorority houses, but we really needed a permanent meeting place for the students.

One evening when Bill was driving home from the campus, he felt impressed by the Lord to visit a house, patterned after a beautiful Moorish castle, that had been for sale for more than a year. It was located across the road from UCLA—three minutes from the heart of the campus. He learned that Miss Mears had been interested in the house, so he called her to be sure that we would not be interfering with her plans. Miss Mears assured him that she was no longer interested in buying but would like to see it again. Arrangements were made with the owner, and we went together to look at this lovely home.

When Miss Mears saw the house, her former enthusiasm was rekindled. She approached us with the suggestion that if we would take the responsibility of running the home, she would purchase it and then together we would share the cost of maintenance and other expenses. The house, built in an H shape, would provide both Miss Mears and us with private living areas, and the centrally located dining area would allow us to share our meals together and entertain together or separately as we wished.

Again I found myself with an exuberant husband and many personal doubts as to the proposed plans. I wasn't sure that two women, no matter how much they loved each other, could be compatible under the same roof, even in a house as large and elegant as this one. I was excited, however, that my dream had come true—the dream of living in Bel Air and enjoying so much of the beauty of material things, even though they belonged mostly to Miss Mears. I was enthusiastic, too, about the opportunity to learn as much as I possibly could from this great woman whom God was using so mightily.

The house would also afford a great opportunity to apply my home-economics training. In order to keep it running smoothly and to entertain in the fashion we all desired, I would need to seek information constantly on how to be the perfect hostess. I wanted to do the best job possible and really learn from managing the house. After settling into our new home, we dedicated the house to the Lord and asked Him to use it in a special way for His glory.

Up until that time I had worked full time on campus, but now much of my attention turned to the home. There was much to be done—refurbishing involved shopping for draperies, enhancing the decor, and spending the greater part of one full day a week arranging flowers. We had a beautiful garden and lots of cut flowers in every season. Miss Mears had an epergne on the dining-room table which needed six to eight dozen flowers, and vases in the living room in which no less than two dozen long-stemmed flowers would do. I enjoyed working in the house because I was learning so much in addition to having a tremendous opportunity for self-expression.

At the same time, I was not finding the fulfillment which I knew on campus. Desiring to stay close to my husband's work, yet enjoying my home and the expression I had there, posed a problem for me. Trying to determine each day whether I would go to campus to minister to students or stay at home was a constant battle. In my frustration, I knew that I was not doing an adequate job with either.

This dilemma quickly resolved itself with the appearance of our first child. Now the decision was made for me. I would stay home and say no to other demands on my time.

At first it was fun to be home all the time, to be free from the meetings, to be free to be a mother and a wife. However, my opinion of freedom changed after a few months, but there was no way to reverse my responsibilities.

Needing and wanting an outlet, I managed to resume meeting with the students. Often I would take Zac in the car bed and give him a bottle in the backseat. When he became a toddler I would put his tricycle in the back of the car so he could play and ride in the park while I was meeting with the students. Or, as an alternative, I would have the students come to our home if they had time between classes.

After our second son was born, my responsibilities in the house increased again. Our housekeeper suddenly left without notice. Because of the students who were living with us and the many who were in and out constantly, she had found the housework too strenuous.

When she left, I comforted myself with the thought that new help would not be hard to get and perhaps taking care of the house entirely by myself would be an interesting challenge. Each week hundreds of students were crowding into the house for all kinds of meetings, and many were finding new life in Christ. But keeping the house clean, organizing refreshments, and being a good hostess was a full-time job, as was being an attentive, available wife and mother.

After three weeks the challenge lost its aura, and I found myself physically and emotionally drained. My daily routine emerged as a monotonous and exhaustingly laborious job. I thought that my answer would come in the form of domestic help, but none was available. Because the house was the culprit which was causing all my dissatisfaction and emotional depression, I saw no other solution but to leave.

Repeatedly I would say to Bill, "Honey, we've just got to move. I can't stand this house any longer. All day long I clean, cook, and watch the children, and I can't take it any more. It's too much."

Although he listened to me, he did not see the house as I did. To him our "castle" was an asset to the ministry. The location, the size, and the accessibility were advantages, not disadvantages, and God was obviously using our home.

After months of being filled with anxiety and frustration, I began to wonder if I should seek professional counsel. As I harbored my discontent about the house and the work I had to do, my frustration and dissatisfaction mushroomed to other areas of my life. Soon my husband, my children, Miss Mears, and the students were as irritating to me as the house itself. I felt locked in a dull, monotonous, laborious existence without a key.

This beautiful house. A successful husband. A profitable ministry. Wasn't this everything I'd desired and worked for? But my life was far from being fulfilled. I was frustrated, discouraged, confused, and irritable. This wasn't fulfillment. There had to be more to life than what I was experiencing.

# 2 The D.D.Ds

By this time I was in my early thirties and I knew that if I didn't find a solution, and not just a compromise, I was going to be a very dissatisfied woman for an awfully long time. For several years I believed the boredom and frustration which I experienced with my daily household responsibilities were unique to me. However, I have come to realize that the lack of fulfillment which I faced is as critical a problem to today's woman as it was to me at that time. And the solution I found is just as applicable today as it was then.

In the early 1960s, Betty Friedan's book *The Feminine Mystique* became a best seller and formally popularized the topic into a movement. In response to her book, practically every women's magazine contained articles concerning analysis of the problem. They posed many questions and offered few answers.

It was during this time that I began to share with women's groups, and particularly pastors' wives, my own personal search concerning this lack of fulfillment. At the risk of seeming very naive, immature, and scripturally uninformed, I openly admitted the problems and defeats which I had experienced and more important, the solutions which God had given me. I have learned to cast all my cares upon the Lord because I have the absolute assurance that He cares for me and will satisfy my every need when I trust and obey Him. I have come to realize that God's Word contains the answer to every problem which I or anyone else might ever face. The result was that I couldn't begin to fill the requests for speaking engagements.

It was tremendously satisfying to hear other women say, "Thank you for admitting your weaknesses and sharing the answers which God has given you." From this response I began to realize that sharing these solutions to help others made my difficult experiences seem worthwhile.

Today the homemaker's problem of boredom and lack of fulfillment has been discussed by psychologists, sociologists, educators, and many ministers. An organization has been formed that is devoted to liberating woman from the drudgery of her homemaking responsibilities and giving her status equal to that of man. Yet despite the frankness in the marketplace of ideas and the apparent solutions and alternatives to homemaking, the question still remains the same: Why does the status of Mrs. and Mom present barriers to being a happy, satisfied woman?

Most women with whom I talk are dedicated to their families and are conscientious in their home responsibilities. In many ways, most wives and mothers are grateful for their families and their homes and many welcome the responsibilities of being both wife and mother. But ironically those same responsibilities which bring great blessing to many women can cripple and make them bitter and resentful, just as they had done to me.

As I have had opportunities to counsel and speak with women from different walks of life, I have found that the problems women face today are common ground.

Frequently the young career woman, who has received a good education and found satisfaction in developing personal expertise, questions whether she should concern herself with marriage at all. Although she desires to be married eventually, she is afraid of losing her identity in her husband and children. She is wary of becoming absorbed in the routine of homemaking and of failing to develop herself to the degree she might otherwise be able to do. Basically she asks, "Can I really be fulfilled if I'm not doing that which challenges me intellectually?"

For example, one twenty-four-year-old, with her wedding only two months away, remorsefully commented:

> His life-style will improve. He'll have me to do the cooking and cleaning. All of his physical needs will be met so that he can advance in his career with minimal outside hindrance, while I will be deterred because of my home responsibilities. I know that if we both continue in our professions, he will be freer than I to take advantage of a promotion and subsequent job transfer.

Looking forward to her marriage, yet acknowledging one of the "inevitable" ramifications of being a wife, another young bride-to-be remarked, "I guess I won't be able to travel now."

Tragically, many women simply resign themselves to marriage, which they view as second-class status, rather than face living alone.

The young homemaker with small children finds her circumstances quite different, yet her desire to be her own person is identical to that of a career woman. However, young mothers have very little uninterrupted time to pursue activities that interest them. As one woman communicated, "Everything I do, I need to redo daily. I am plagued with the D.D.D.s—dishes, diapers, and dust. Instead of having them finished and accomplished, there is a never-ending list of things to do and to do over again."

A very capable friend once told me:

> I went through college with scholarships and good grades.
> But when I became a mother there was no one to reward
> me with A's for doing the dishes or scholarships for mak-
> ing beds. The world I was used to and thoroughly en-
> joyed was no longer there saying, "You're doing a good
> job, Mary, keep it up."

Many women feel guilty about seeking employment because
they don't want to put their children in day-care centers. Often
private sitters are too expensive, so the mothers have nowhere
to turn but back to their housework. It isn't long before they
begin to feel that they are playing a martyr's role, and they
resent it.

I understand the feeling of martyrdom, for it affected me
when our children were small and the labor of taking care of
the household needs was at its height. My husband was experiencing one of the most exciting times of his life, and due to
the growth of our ministry, it was necessary that he travel
throughout the country for weeks at a time. However, Campus
Crusade's limited funds made it impossible for me to travel with
him. I longed to go with him and be involved in the activities
that seemed so glamorous, but it just wasn't possible.

One Christmas season we were at a party where Dr. and
Mrs. Louis Evans, Sr., were present. Dr. Evans was the pastor
of Hollywood Presbyterian Church, where Bill and I became
Christians and where we both experienced so much spiritual
growth. In talking with them, I learned that Mrs. Evans was
accompanying her husband on a tour to Japan. A little envious,
I said longingly, "Oh, it must be wonderful to travel with your
husband!"

Putting her arm around my shoulders she lovingly said, "Yes,
my dear, it is wonderful to travel with my husband. This is one
of the compensations of my age. But there have been compen-

sations with every age." Thanks to Mrs. Evans, I left that party with an encouraging bit of wisdom for a frustrating time in my life.

A mother who has little contact outside her home and finds little challenge in homemaking may tend to feel lonely and forgotten. If relations are strained between her and her husband, she doesn't receive his appreciation. Often this causes her to feel taken for granted and her job as homemaker seems especially unfulfilling.

Some mothers have determined that they are not going to stay at home, and so they enter the work force as professionals or unskilled laborers, depending upon their training. On the front page of the *Wall Street Journal,* a story told of the adjustments a woman advertising executive, who was also a wife and mother, was making to maintain her two careers.

She explained that with her husband's help they had worked out a satisfactory arrangement to care for their home and children and still function efficiently in their work. She said occasionally there were complications, such as who would pick the children up from school or which parent would attend to the child if a baby-sitter was not available. She pointed out, however, that this kind of an arrangement was not without its frustrations and crises. And when they got down to the very basics of the matter, she said, the success of maintaining two careers and operating a home depended upon the availability of a good baby-sitter.

All jobs are not glamorous and a working mother may also have to face the problems which a boring, unrewarding job holds. These negatives are often coupled with the dissatisfaction that comes from having time to do only the laborious tasks at home and from being unable to really have fun with her home and children.

The years of involvement with home and ministry have caused me to identify with overcommitment and the problems unique to a two-career woman. One incident in particular gives me a great understanding of the problems the career woman must face.

One hot, humid summer in Minnesota during a Campus Crusade Staff Training, Bill told ten guests, "We are going to revise the staff manual." Hearing his intentions about the manual which I had originally edited, I countered with, "We are?"

Bill replied, "Yes, dear, I've been intending to tell you. I have decided the revisions are necessary. So you and the children (ages two and six) can remain here and you and a secretary can work on it during the two weeks I am away. Then you can drive to California to meet me."

I liked the challenge of completing the manual and knew it would be an aid to our staff, but I also wanted the fun of entertaining the children and going with Bill. It wasn't long after Bill left that I began to feel the strain of balancing my work for Campus Crusade and my responsibilities as a mother. It was a great relief when the manual was finally finished a year later, for because of my attitude the entire project had been accomplished under pressure.

The working woman with children is a candidate for increased turmoil in her life, as I was very much aware after working on that manual, because many times she has difficulty in maintaining a singleness of mind and purpose. For when she is at work, she may find herself concentrating on what needs to be done at home, and when she's home, she may find her mind focusing on office responsibilities.

Whether a woman is a full-time homemaker or combines a career with family responsibilities, before she can believe it, she finds her small babies are lanky, independent teenagers. With this metamorphosis, she gladly accepts an eased work load, but now finds her struggle is more emotional than physical.

Today there are many obstacles which seriously interfere with communication between a child and a parent. Sometimes these problems even come through the institutions to which we send our children. An instance which was especially distressing to me was when our oldest son came home from high school to share what the students had been told in the classroom: "Don't go home and tell your parents about the racial conflicts and incidents of violence at school. They can't do anything about them; we can solve our own problems."

A friend of mine who has a teenage daughter shared the difficulties she was facing. This mother had discovered her daughter leaving the house late at night to take drugs with friends. In an attempt to discipline her, both she and her husband took the girl's privileges away. In spite of their efforts, the girl continued to meet with her friends. In desperation, the parents locked her in her room, but she climbed out her bedroom window. The daughter, in a fit of anger, told her mother, "If I want to take drugs, there is not one single thing you or anyone else can do about it."

The mother was shocked at her daughter's flagrant disobedience and alarmed with her activities, but she also realized that there really wasn't anything she could physically do to prevent her daughter from taking drugs.

I believe the family goes through its greatest time of testing and the mother through her greatest period of stress during the children's teenage years. The emotional strain on a woman during this time most often takes its toll on a woman's creativity and contributes to making her say, "What's the use?" As a result, when she's distraught, she can't meet the needs of her husband and children.

The older homemaker with grown children has frustrations unique to her situation. In discusing one of the major pitfalls of this age group, a good friend quickly identified the problem and offered her caution.

Her remark came at a time when I wanted the challenge of developing myself but still had the responsibilities of my teenage children who needed my attention. My friend said:

> When my children were growing up, I thought they need-
> ed a pal. So I rode horses, went swimming, and partici-
> pated in the activities children enjoy. However, now my
> children are grown and they don't need me, and, of
> course, they don't want me following them around. I am
> completely alone and have no real expertise on which to
> build a career or make any significant contribution. Don't
> neglect your children, but at the same time develop some
> degree of expertise while you can. When you get to be
> fifty years old, people aren't interested in the experience
> you gained as a twenty-one-year-old. People are more
> tolerant of a lack of ability at a young age than they are
> when you are mature.

I have come to see the wisdom of this advice as I've watched many women experiencing a great lack of fulfillment and facing the question "What do I do now?"

Because my children are now away from home for the first time in years, I have no one demanding my attention or re-questing I be at a certain place at a certain hour. Fortunately, I have expression through the ministry of Campus Crusade, and my husband is very attentive and considerate of my needs.

One of the paradoxes of this age is that, while a woman may have the time and desire to exercise a degree of independence, she usually finds herself seeking security from her husband. However, a wife may often find her husband is involved in the successful fulfillment of his dreams, and he is completely satu-rated in his work. In these circumstances, husbands have little time to consider the frustrations of their wives.

Unfortunately, many women face the tragic fact that they have neglected to maintain a close relationship with their mate during the difficult trials of their children's teenage years. Then when they truly desire security, they've lost their husband's close companionship.

In his counsel for married couples, Dr. Henry Brandt, a well-known Christian psychologist, says:

> The normal course of events in family living means you're going to end up right where you've started—just the two of you—so you had better stay friends. And if you aren't friends, you better make friends. . . . Maintain that relationship as husband and wife because that is the enduring relationship. Parenthood goes its own way, but husband/wife relationships remain.

But whatever period of life a woman is in—with the children gone, in the process of growing up or still arriving, with her mind on her career or on her household—the desire to develop her person, the dissatisfaction and lack of fulfillment are still easily identified as common ground for women. The homemaker's predicament, unfortunately, is one that has far-reaching ramifications. If she is dissatisfied at home, she can negatively influence a vast number of people including her husband, her children, and those in her church and community.

I have observed the effects of a wife's negative attitude in other homes and have experienced a bit of it myself. In my case, I've found that my husband, who is not only my lover but also my minister and counselor, has on occasion helped me realize that my disposition was not the most pleasing to him or to the family. I have not enjoyed having him point out those times, and I may have come to my own defense, but I have known in my heart he was right. I am grateful for a husband who is strong enough not to tolerate inconsistencies that would affect our family and who will point out where I'm wrong with the instruction and encouragement I need to change.

But each family lives its life differently, and each woman deals with her personal dissatisfaction in her own way. Unfortunately, some women have opted for some ineffective ways out.

# 3 Table of Spiritual Valence

In searching for fulfillment, one woman's description of her experience echoes that of many:

> As a child, I thought when I got to high school that would be the "ultimate." There I would find happiness. When I got to high school, I thought surely the great joy of life comes in college. But when I got to college, it seemed happiness would not come until I got in the right sorority. After joining the "best house," I determined genuine satisfaction was only possible when I found the right man to marry. But after the wedding, my desire for fulfillment centered in living in the right house in the right section of the city. After moving into our new home, I looked forward to having a child and being fulfilled as a mother. The day the baby was christened we had an extravagant party at our house. After the guests had left, I thought, *Now where else can I go for the fulfillment which continues to elude me?* A few years later I separated from

my husband and we were divorced, and I began to realize
there was no place to go.

Whether we are looking to major events or material plea-
sures of life to give us a sense of purpose and fulfillment, we
find ourselves still unsatisfied and searching. A friend tells the
story of a woman in this situation who had come for counsel.
She believed having a new stove would help her find satisfaction
at home. So to please her, her husband saved his money and
bought her a stove for Christmas. Absolutely delighted, she
thought, *I can bake all I want and everything will turn out all
right.*

After three weeks, she discovered the refrigerator wasn't
functioning properly and she couldn't store the things she was
baking. When she discussed the problem with her husband, he
consented to buy a new refrigerator on time payments.

As they enjoyed their new stove and refrigerator, they no-
ticed how shabby the kitchen looked. So they splurged again
and redecorated the kitchen.

In the course of entertaining, they would bring their guests
into the prettiest room in the house—the kitchen. However,
they did not want to entertain their guests there so they decided
to redo their living room and make it as nice as the kitchen.

Soon their interior decorating went from the living room to
the bedrooms until their whole house was completely refurbished. Finally, after a few months, their home was beautiful
but they didn't have ten cents to spare to purchase an ice-cream
cone.

The price of their extravagances took its toll not only on
their pocketbook but also on their relationship. Although they
did not realize what had happened because of their strained
finances, they were soon at each other's throats and in a psychologist's office asking, "What's gone wrong with our marriage?"

Having an abundance of money isn't the key to fulfillment, either. I have known individuals who have said, "I cannot understand why people who have money are not happy." And yet, some of the most miserable people are those who have money—a lot of money.

On the other hand, I know some who say, "I would be happy if I didn't have anything." One woman I know gives everything away except a meager amount on which to live because she believes happier people are those who have less money on which to live. She reached that conclusion because she doesn't know anyone in her affluent station of life who is happy.

Other women try to find fulfillment by serving in a philanthropic organization or helping deprived individuals. It's wonderful to be able to have the time, finances, energy—and possibly even prestige and influence to exert for needy organizations. But when this is our only avenue to contentment and finding fulfillment, it, too, brings emptiness, frustration, and dissatisfaction.

Many times the career woman is looking for fulfillment in making a name for herself and excelling over those with whom she is working. But as many women who have made it to the top know, there still is that lack of heartfelt satisfaction.

Don't misunderstand. There is nothing wrong with material possessions. There is nothing wrong with desiring position or achievement in life. But these temporal goals for which we strive bring only temporary fulfillment and happiness. We are like children with a short attention span, who play with a toy for a while, but soon leave it for something else.

Somehow this doesn't fit in with the fact that God has promised us a full and meaningful life—yes, an abundant, purposeful life. God wishes for us to be content as individuals—fulfilled as women, wives, and mothers. In John 10:10 Jesus promised, ". . . I came that they might have life, and might have it abundantly"—that life might be full and meaningful.

But, if God has promised us a meaningful life, why are women of all ages and statures of life bored and unfulfilled? The problem lies in our not realizing that only He can fill that personal void—not people, not circumstances, not material possessions. Either we have not understood God's perspective or we have failed to trust God and follow His way. Such was my situation.

I consider myself a very practical-minded person. In college, I minored in chemistry and everything had to be very practical and workable to me. This was one reason I questioned Christianity. I had never understood the practical, workable, everyday implications of Christianity. After graduating from college, I made that visit to Bill in Los Angeles. He was concerned about my uncertainty with Christianity and suggested I see Dr. Henrietta Mears, the woman who had answered many of his questions.

At our first meeting Miss Mears mentioned she had taught chemistry in Minneapolis and understood how I was thinking. Using terminology with which I was very familiar, she explained to me from the Bible that God loves me. She said that if I had been the only person in all the world, God would have done everything He could to reveal Himself to me. From the Bible she showed me that God had a plan and purpose for me which could result in a full and meaningful life. However, before I could know that plan and purpose, it was necessary for me to know God.

Then she explained that, just as a person who enters a chemistry laboratory to perform a chemical experiment follows the table of chemical valence, so it is necessary to enter God's laboratory and follow His formula in order to know Him. She continued to explain that the basic reason man does not know God is that man is sinful and separated from God.

When she said that all people are basically sinful, I knew she was not including me. My reaction was, "Speak for yourself, please; that doesn't apply to me—I have worked at this business of being a good girl."

Then she showed me Romans 3:23 which states, "For all have sinned and fall short of the glory of God." She explained that sin is simply falling short of God's best or God's perfection, and I realized that this was my daily experience.

I recalled how I had kept lists of areas of my life that needed to be worked on—such as being more loving to people, more considerate, more helpful, or neater. But it wasn't long before I realized my self-efforts could not make me perfect. Once I heard a person say that you can tell a great deal about an individual's character by the condition of her dresser drawers. So I cleaned all my drawers, the closet, and the chest. After taking a shower to refresh myself from my dirty work, I pulled the cosmetic drawer too hard and everything fell out, scattering in all directions. That ended my attempt to be neat as well as my list making. My conclusion was, "I am as I am and people will have to accept me this way."

Miss Mears went on to show me Romans 6:23 "For the wages [meaning payment or salary or results] of sin [spiritual separation from God] is death [meaning a continued spiritual separation]; but the free gift of God is eternal life in Christ Jesus our Lord."

At this time I began to consider who I thought Jesus Christ was. Miss Mears suggested there were several facts about Jesus Christ which were important to know. He lived the only perfect life that had ever been lived. He did things no other man had ever done. He was the greatest teacher who ever lived. He did more for civilization than any other individual. He actually died on the cross for our sins, and He is the Son of God who lives today.

I had to admit that I didn't know very much about Jesus Christ. But statements which she pointed out to me that Jesus had made helped me understand what I had missed before. "I and the Father are one" (John 10:30). He said, "He who has seen Me has seen the Father" (John 14:9). And, ". . . I am the way, and the truth, and the life; no one comes to the Father, but through Me" (John 14:6). I came to the conclusion that Jesus was either who He claimed to be—God—or the Bible was not true. And I couldn't believe a person who had done so much for mankind and who, after two thousand years, most people believe to be the greatest person who ever lived, could be a fraud.

I knew that I had tried to live a good life. I had maintained a high moral standard, and I had been active in church. In spite of this, I knew I did not know God in a vital, personal way. The light began to dawn that perhaps Jesus Christ was the element I needed in my formula.

So I said, "If Jesus Christ is the way, then how does one get to know Him?" Dr. Mears responded by pointing out to me God's promise from Revelation 3:20. Christ says, "Behold, I stand at the door and knock; if any one hears My voice and opens the door, I will come in to him. . . ." Then she pointed out to me, "But as many as received Him, to them He gave the right to become children of God, even to those who believe in His name" (John 1:12).

It is not enough to just glibly make a profession of receiving Christ. Many times I had sung "Into my heart, Lord Jesus, come in today, come in to stay." At those times I had really meant it, and that act seemed to help for a day or two, yet my life had not permanently changed. Miss Mears explained that believing in Him means to trust in, to cling to, to rely upon Him, and that receiving Christ was simply a matter of turning myself—my will, emotions, and intellect—completely over to Him and inviting Him to take control of my life.

Miss Mears also challenged me to be sure that Christ was in my life. If what she told me was true, I knew that I had nothing to lose and everything to gain. So we bowed our heads together and I asked Christ, once and for all, to come into my heart.

Many people are plagued with doubts as to whether or not they are Christians. Many go through the motions of receiving Christ over and over again. Many are not sure whether or not they have ever received Christ. Let me suggest a solution.

If you are not sure of your relationship with God, you should make sure. All you need to do is prayerfully confess to God that you realize you are separated from Him because of your attitude of self-sufficiency or deliberate disobedience, which the Bible calls sin. Ask sincerely that Jesus Christ come into your heart and take control of your life. Confess any known sin and simply ask God to make you the person He would want you to be. The words matter little—the attitude of your heart is what is important.

The following is a suggested prayer:

Lord Jesus, I need You. Thank You for dying on the cross for my sins. I open the door of my life and receive You as my Savior and Lord. Thank You for forgiving my sins and giving me eternal life. Take control of the throne of my life. Make me the kind of person You want me to be.

Does this prayer express the desire of your heart? Would you like to pray this prayer right now? Take time to read it again and meditate upon how the prayer applies to you. Pray it right now so that you can be sure that Christ is in your life.

Did you sincerely ask Jesus Christ to come into your heart? If you did, where is He right now? He is in your heart, for He promised and He does not lie. If you ask Him to come into your heart to take control of your life—your will, emotions, and intellect—He will do just that. Remember, Jesus promised, "Behold, I stand at the door and knock; if any one hears My voice and opens the door, I will come in to him . . ." (Revelation 3:20).

The change which follows this initial act may be sudden or gradual, according to one's personality. Do not seek or be confused by an emotional experience. Emotions will come and go. Place your faith in the faithfulness of God and the fact of His Word.

And the witness is this, that God has given us eternal life, and this life is in His Son. He who has the Son has the life (right now); he who does not have the Son of God does not have the life. These things I have written to you who believe in the name of the Son of God, in order that you may know that you have eternal life (1 John 5:11-13).

As it was for me, so it will be true for you. Receiving Christ and knowing God personally is the beginning of being fulfilled as an individual—being content within yourself.

Knowing Christ adds a totally new dimension to life. He gives direction and connects you with the most powerful force in all the world—God. Only Christ can produce in you those qualities which you desire, and again, only Jesus Christ can enable you to do and be more than your mind can possibly comprehend. How is this possible? Begin with the step of faith by placing your trust in Him, and as you continue to trust Him, what I and millions of others have experienced will become a reality to you.

Just as the use of the table of chemical valence when followed in the chemical laboratory will produce a predictable result, so will the application of God's formulas found in His Word enable an individual to reach his fullest potential for such a time as this.

# 4 Looking Up

To me there were many exciting things about receiving Christ: I knew that my prayers were now heard and I experienced answers. My life began to take a new direction. Areas of my life that I had tried to improve now seemed in control. I knew my sins were forgiven, I had eternal life, and I had the promise from Jesus that my life would be full and meaningful. However, when I found myself in my "Moorish castle" with my routine, boring, domestic situation, it hardly seemed that Jesus was fulfilling that last promise. At times I asked myself, *Where is the reality of being a Christian in this situation?*

I may have been living in Bel Air, but it was also true that I had never felt so abused before. It seemed people were taking advantage of me and expecting more than I was physically capable of doing. I was also resentful because I knew I could accomplish more significant things and participate in more glamorous activities than being a housekeeper.

Determined something had to change, I told my husband on different occasions about my discouragement and physical exhaustion. Invariably he would say, "Now, honey, how much time have you spent reading your Bible and praying today? Did you really take time to be alone with the Lord?"

After listening to his solution a few times, I wanted to throw the Bible at him. I didn't need the Bible, in my opinion. I needed a maid or a change in our domestic situation.

Desperately I prayed God would give me an answer. A few weeks later we were invited to a college conference at which Bill was to speak. He suggested it would be a good opportunity for me to rest and relax, so I accepted the invitation with much enthusiasm. Among the many seminars available to the participants, one was particularly significant to me. The speaker made the statement, "Dissatisfaction and frustration are not of God. If we are dissatisfied or frustrated about something, we should ask God what is causing us to be that way and then ask Him to remove it. If He doesn't remove it, we are to ask what He wants us to learn from that situation."

After hearing that statement, I decided to pray that God would take us out of that house. But when nobody became excited about the idea, I realized that God was going to leave me there to teach me something even though I wasn't sure I wanted to learn it. However, a few days later, alone in the quiet of our bedroom, I knelt at the window seat in prayer and submitted my will to Him. My prayer was, "Lord, if You're going to leave me here in this house, with these circumstances, You will have to make me willing to be made willing to learn what You want me to learn."

That prayer changed the course of my life, for soon after I became aware of one very important concept I had missed before: my attitude—not my circumstances—was what was making me unhappy. At last I was willing to learn the things God wanted to teach me.

It is important to know that, when we become willing to learn, God leads us to a person, a book, a portion of Scripture, or something that begins to unfold the truth He wishes to apply in our lives.

Step by step God began to give me answers to my problems and frustrations. In a conversation with a friend, she remarked, "God doesn't need my ability, He wants my availability." So I began making myself available. Talking with God I often had to say, "I'm available to wash these dishes. I'm available to prepare these meals. Lord, I'm available to do anything You want me to do."

Bill began to emphasize 1 Thessalonians 5:18 in his teaching. Though I had heard many times, "In everything give thanks; for this is God's will for you in Christ Jesus." I decided to begin to apply it. I began to thank God for diapers, for dishes, dinners, interruptions, people, and the many tedious tasks I had to do.

In the beginning it wasn't easy to be available or to give thanks. Many times through tears I tried to practice what I had learned. Inevitably, the most difficult time to apply these new truths occurred every Tuesday night.

In our home we held College Life meetings, at which a message about Jesus Christ would be given. Bill and the staff living with us would move all the furniture out of the way and students would be jam-packed in the dining room, the two halls, the living room, and up into a little room which served as a study.

Most of the time while the students were there, I had to be in the kitchen getting the refreshments, and I resented it terribly. I wanted to have the glamour of being in the forefront as the hostess—helping to make the announcements, introducing the students, and talking to them personally about Jesus Christ. Many times as I was getting the refreshments, I would complain, "Now, Lord, I could lead these students to Christ in half the time these new staff members could. They ought to be in here getting these refreshments, and I ought to be out there."

Yet, in my heart I knew that this was right—I knew they needed the training, so I tried to apply my new truth: "Thank You, Father, for the privilege of getting these refreshments. Thank You that I can serve You in this kitchen. I may not meet one student tonight, but thank You for the privilege of preparing these refreshments for them."

Little by little, I began to experience real joy—God-given joy—in preparing the punch and the cookies for Him.

Then I began to do everything for the Lord. I washed diapers for Jesus. I mopped floors for Jesus. I cleaned house for Jesus— not for Campus Crusade, not for Bill Bright, not for Henrietta Mears, not for my family—but I was doing it for Jesus. It amazed me to gradually see the drudgery and the humdrum work turn into activities which had meaning and new purpose. I started in a new way to use the creative mind God had given me, and I began to get organized.

After a few weeks, the house was running like clockwork. God had sent enough domestic help to relieve me of some of the responsibility. At the same time, I found I could do more than one task at a time. By changing my negative attitude, I found I had creative energy I hadn't known I had. I truly began to enjoy my home, to accept it as my ministry, and I was challenged to reach my greatest personal potential right there.

Often when students came for counseling, they would say, "Isn't there something I can do to help?" I found I could mend clothes or sew on buttons and they could iron handkerchiefs or tablecloths while I counseled with them. If I was getting dinner, I'd invite them into the kitchen and continue to prepare my meals as I was counseling. Of course, there were times when that was not at all appropriate. I found, however, that by allowing them to help, they felt themselves to be a greater part of my life. Talking and sharing with each other was even more casual

and meaningful as we worked together. When they offered to
help, I learned to accept their help. I soon had more time to be
on the campus working with the students than I had when
there was full-time help.

What was the difference? My attitude had changed. I had
learned that the Lord was my source of joy, peace, and happiness—not my circumstances, or the way people treated me.

The reason I can now say that joy is in the Lord is that I
know that wherever He puts me, I can be the most productive.
Because I know I am doing exactly what He wants me to do,
I can experience great satisfaction and joy.

God gives us much assurance from His Word that He is in
control of our circumstances. In Philippians 2:13 we learn, "It
is God who is at work in you, both to will and to work for His
good pleasure." I have come to realize that as I submit my will
to the Lord, He is not going to allow me to make a mistake. If
He plants in me the desire to accomplish a task, He will also
give me the necessary power to do it.

In one of the guiding verses of my life, Psalms 37:5, we are
told, "Commit your way to the LORD, Trust also in Him, and
He will do it." The first seven verses of Psalm 37 give us clear
direction and encouragement: Fret not because of evildoers; do
not worry, or actually, stop worrying; don't be overly concerned because of evildoers; but delight in the Lord and He'll
give you the desires of your heart.

Also, in Proverbs 3:5, 6 we are told, ". . . lean not unto thine
own understanding. In all thy ways acknowledge him, and he
shall direct thy paths" (KJV). These verses of Scripture have
been mainstays to me as I have trusted Him to guide me in the
right direction.

I have learned that when I look at my circumstances, it is
easy to become discouraged and defeated, for I am not making
myself available to God. But Scripture tells us the solution:
"Set your mind on the things above, not on the things that are

on earth. For you have died and your life is hidden with Christ in God" (Colossians 3:2, 3). I realize from these verses that I am to look to Christ in every kind of situation—to set my sights and affection on Him, and then I will have victory.

Applying this concept became real when guests arrived unexpectedly in the midst of an overloaded daily schedule. After seating her guests, Miss Mears would often appear at the spot where I was working and say, "Honey, would you mind serving a little pot of tea to the committee meeting?"

There had been times when I had happily replied, "I'd love to," but in my heart I was saying, *Why doesn't she get her own cup of tea?* Now I found that my response was a genuine "I would be happy to," no matter what the inconvenience, because I was available to God.

Through many circumstances such as this I began to accept interruptions and previously irritating situations as God's way of telling me what He wanted me to do. Little by little I began to understand the reality of the Christ-controlled life. I find the application of this principle just as important now as when I first learned it a number of years ago.

We determine in our own minds whether or not we are going to be upset and how we are going to react to a situation. Jesus said, "Let not your heart be troubled. You are trusting God, now trust in me" (John 14:1 LB). We should remember Jesus' admonition, "Don't let your heart be troubled." When disappointing news comes, we must strive to develop the habit of quickly saying to the Lord, "I trust You. I will not let my heart be troubled."

Often people say, "Don't tell me about saying thank you to God for a situation or a circumstance in life. You don't have the problems I have." That was what one woman remarked to a friend of mine whose first husband had died of cancer. My friend was teaching a class on this principle and one of the women in attendance became very critical.

The teacher quizzed the woman and learned that she was bitter because her husband was dying of cancer. My friend explained to her how God had worked uniquely in her own life as a result of her husband's death. She told how her first husband had prayed that God would bring her a loving Christian man who would be a good husband to her and a good father to her nine-year-old son. Of course, she wasn't interested in another person and only wanted her husband to be well. Yet, a few years after his death, God sent a loving Christian man into her life who desired to enter Christian work, which had also been her desire.

She now had a second husband, who was the absolute delight of her life and a tremendous father to her son, as well as the opportunity to give full time to teaching others the reality of God in their personal lives. The other woman, of course, was stunned to think she was talking to someone who had gone through a circumstance similar to hers and had seen God sovereignly use that in her life.

I shall never forget the words of Dale Evans Rogers as she spoke at a congressional-wives' prayer breakfast. Her daughter, Debbie, had been killed in a bus accident, and this was her first speaking engagement since the accident. We were all concerned about Dale and Roy and grieved with them, but she victoriously opened her remarks with, "Ladies, I'm here to tell you that God is real. I know." From that moment on, everybody knew that what Dale had to say about God was real in her life.

Today, the books of Dale Evans Rogers are in great demand and her ministry is strong because people realize she has experienced what she's talking about.

So many times we want to escape the character building that God wants to perform in our lives. We would like to take shortcuts to becoming the total person we want to be. We would like to escape the difficulties, and yet, these are the situations through which God becomes a reality in our lives.

Trying circumstances are teaching ground. I've begun to realize that as we face unpleasant difficulties and situations, this is the time when God is giving us a message that we can share with others. Many times we would like to be of help to other people; we would like to have an outstanding ministry. But before we can have a ministry, we must have a message. How do we develop a message? By experiencing the reality of God in all kinds of situations. And so, even though we don't ask for them, as unpleasant and hard times come, we can learn to thank God because He will use them to our betterment.

He will take those circumstances, which from a human standpoint are tragic, chaotic, and frustrating, and make them into that which is meaningful, building, and constructive. He will use them to conform us to the image of Christ and make us into the persons we desire to be.

As long as we resist God's will and remain bitter, discouraged, and angry, God cannot do His work in our lives. But as we submit and thank Him, we are able to learn the lessons which He wants us to know. This is a giant step toward becoming fulfilled as Christians.

God works in us "both to will and to do His good pleasure" (*see* Philippians 2:13) to cause us to be conformed to the image of Christ and bring honor and glory to Him. Even in the beginning of the Scriptures, we are told God brought us into existence to have fellowship with Himself and to be an honor to Him.

God wants us to willingly present ourselves to Him as we are told in Romans 12:1: "I beseech you therefore, brethren . . . that ye present your bodies a living sacrifice, holy, acceptable unto God, which is your reasonable service" (KJV). As this verse points out, it is the only reasonable and intelligent thing for us to do. We were made for God, and we cannot operate properly without Him. Just as it is only reasonable that we put gasoline rather than water into the tank of a car, so it is only reasonable that we submit to God, for that is the way in which we operate best.

The second verse of Romans 12 says, "Do not be conformed to this world, but be transformed by the renewing of your mind, that you may prove what the will of God is, that which is good and acceptable and perfect." We are to set our minds on Him, and as we make ourselves available to Him, He will show us His good and perfect will for our lives. We do not have to try to struggle to live the Christian life. We are only to trust and obey Him. God makes it clear that He does not want us to work for Him—He doesn't even need our help. He just wants us to let Him live His life in and through us. And the way He has made this possible is through the enabling of the Holy Spirit.

It was only as I realized that happiness depended upon my relationship to God and my availability to Him that my attitude changed. It didn't matter how much work I had to do, how much confusion I had around me, or how people treated me, now I could look to Jesus as my source of joy, energy, and power, and find that God would give me a contented heart.

As I look back, I wonder what would have happened if I had followed my own desire—if I had insisted we leave that house. I shudder to think of the lessons I would not have learned and the great happiness and satisfaction I would have missed. For I had begun to understand the "something more."

# 5 Something More

Soon after I became a Christian, I began to hear about the Holy Spirit. Although I didn't understand how His ministry related to me, I continued to read my Bible and pray. During this time I was sharing my faith and taking a more active part in my husband's ministry, but I was not seeing much spiritual fruit. After several months of striving to be a Christian, I began to realize there had to be something more to this life in Christ.

I started to understand what that "something more" was all about the summer before I joined Bill full time with Campus Crusade. I attended a women's Christian retreat, and during the conference, I was reminded of the scriptural principle that God demands obedience before He can give blessing (*see* Deuteronomy 11:27). The mention of obedience reminded me of an apology I had never made, which triggered a reminder of two other letters of apology that should have been written but never were. The matters were trivial and so much time had elapsed since the incidents occurred that I tried to put the idea of writing these letters out of my mind.

But every time I would desire to be used by God in someone else's life, I was reminded that He couldn't really use me until I was obedient to what I knew He wanted me to do. Finally, after months of procrastination, I sat down to write those letters. I kept thinking how silly these people were going to think I was, and I didn't want to be embarrassed.

Unable to put my sealed letters in the mailbox, I walked to the prayer chapel to spend time alone with God. I asked Him to show me whether or not this was really what I had to do. I thought surely the willingness to write the letters was sufficient, and maybe it wasn't necessary to mail them. In my prayers, I asked Him to give me one more signal.

As I returned to my room, I overheard a conversation which related specifically to the situation for which I was apologizing. I knew then that I had to mail the letters. While I walked to the mailbox, I had confidence that what I was doing was right, but I wondered if the result of my action would just be embarrassment or if God would really bless my life because I was obedient.

A short time later, I heard a discussion about the Holy Spirit. It was then that I understood that the Holy Spirit had come into my life when I received Jesus Christ as my personal Savior and that He would control and empower my life only as I surrendered my will totally to Him. Looking back on the time I had dropped those letters in the mail, I knew that I had totally surrendered every area of my life to God at that time, and that by faith I could know that He was in control of my life.

The response to my letters indicated there was no significance and the incident could now be forgotten. My mind was totally relieved that I had been obedient to God.

As school began that fall, I spent much of my time meeting with girls, telling them about Jesus Christ. In the first four months, I saw more than fifty of them receive Christ. This in itself gave me the assurance that I was filled with the

Holy Spirit and that God was indeed blessing me for being obedient and surrendering my life to Him. I began to see that I could not live the Christian life but that Christ wanted to live it through me. Since that time, I have learned that Jesus did not come just to be our example but also to give us a whole new quality of life—His indwelling resurrection life. And it is through the power of the Holy Spirit that this new life becomes a reality to us.

The Holy Spirit makes Christianity believable and livable. He makes Christ relevant to us at the dishpan, at the ironing board, in the marketplace, while we're taking care of a sick child or an invalid mother-in-law, or conducting a meeting. He makes Christ as real in those circumstances as He is in the church pew on Sunday morning. If this is not true, there is something wrong with our Christianity.

A student from India once said in criticism of Christians, "They are quite ordinary people professing superordinary power." However, if Christ indwells our lives, and we are controlled by the Holy Spirit, there should be a readily apparent, superordinary quality manifested in our lives.

But how can we be controlled by the Holy Spirit? At the time we receive Jesus Christ as our personal Savior, the Holy Spirit comes to indwell our lives. Some individuals misunderstand and try to imagine a person coming into their lives in bodily form. They are like the little girl who warily remarked, "Daddy, I don't want the Holy Spirit in my life because I'm a little girl, and He won't fit inside of me." The Holy Spirit, however, is spirit, not body, and He indwells our very being—mind, body, and soul.

An illustration which helped me to understand the Holy Spirit in my life concerns a hand and glove:

> What does a glove do for a hand? It adds a bit of warmth, protection, and color. However, it is only as your hand is

slipped into the glove that it performs the task it was created to do. So it is with the Holy Spirit. We are simply the covering for Jesus Christ who lives in our lives through His Holy Spirit.

But there is a difference between being indwelt by the Holy Spirit and controlled by the Holy Spirit. Every Christian is indwelt by the Holy Spirit, but to be controlled by the Holy Spirit, one must completely surrender his life to live in obedience to Christ; only then can one be filled with the Holy Spirit. To be filled means to be empowered and controlled. In Ephesians 5:18, we are commanded, "Do not get drunk with wine, for that is dissipation, but be filled with the Spirit."

God never commands us to do anything that He does not give us the ability to do. He would never command us to be filled with the Holy Spirit without enabling us to be filled. All that we need to do is to receive the fullness of the Holy Spirit by faith and then believe that God will live His life through us.

The placement of the verse commanding us to be filled with the Spirit is very interesting to me. Immediately after this portion, God speaks of relationships with other Christians, husbands, wives, and children. God is so practical. I've come to realize that unless the Holy Spirit is a reality in our lives in our domestic situations, He is not likely to be a reality at all. In Acts 1:8, God promises that we will receive power when the Holy Spirit has come upon us so that we may be His witnesses right where we are. I believe that means especially in our homes.

Letting the Holy Spirit control my life does not necessarily mean that I will experience a high point of emotion or feel exhilarated spiritually or physically 100 percent of the time. Many people become disappointed when they learn that this is not true of the Spirit-filled life. Emotions come and go and cannot be relied upon. We should not allow feelings to affect our relationship with God. We must place our confidence in Him and His promises.

Often our physical health has a definite effect on our feelings. For instance, we may be extremely tired, and because we don't feel exhilarated, we may think we aren't filled with the Spirit. However, the reason we feel the way we do is that we need rest. It may be that we need more physical exercise, or we need to give more attention to a balanced diet.

Our attitudes, however, are a much more reliable gauge in our relationship to God. I clearly saw this one afternoon when I decided to mop the kitchen floor. I had happily gone about the task, but while the floor was drying, our younger son came running into the house with a group of little boys trailing behind him. Each of them wanted a glass of milk, and Brad, without asking, decided he would get it. But while he was pouring the milk, he spilled it on my shiny floor. As he called to me, I found myself saying in a very loud voice, "Get out of the kitchen! I just mopped the floor!" With their eyes wide open, all the boys scurried out, scared because Brad's mother had acted the way she did. I felt terrible.

Now where was the Holy Spirit in this? He was still in my life, but He was not in control of my life. I had exerted my will over His.

To avoid such incidents we occasionally have in our home a "throne room check." It is based on the idea that in each life there is a throne or control center. When the Holy Spirit is in control of our lives, ego or self is dethroned, though self can take control at any moment, as it did in my floor-mopping incident. It does not mean that the Holy Spirit leaves our lives; it means that at that moment He isn't in control. When Christ is in control, there is harmony and peace in an individual's life. When self is in control, there is discord and frustration. We taught this concept to our boys from early childhood, and it is practiced by all of us. Every once in a while, when dispositions are not very pleasant, it is easy to ask, "Who is on the throne?"

One little area in my life continually gives me the opportunity to rely on the Holy Spirit to depend on Him to give me the correct response. My husband is so totally devoted to the Lord and to serving Him that were it not an absolute necessity to eat, he would completely forget about mealtime. After twenty-seven years of marriage, I still have to telephone him every evening to remind him to come home for dinner. I've learned to look at the clock and to gauge my call according to the amount of time it takes him to get his things together at the office and arrive home in time for dinner.

Through the power of the Holy Spirit, I have learned to accept my husband's little idiosyncrasy and to make my call pleasant and even a special pleasure. But from time to time this little practice becomes irritating to me because I decide he should be able to get home for dinner on his own initiative.

When I fail to call him with an attitude of patience and love, I know what to do. My husband calls the corrective action "spiritual breathing." In spiritual breathing we exhale by confessing our sins, and inhale by appropriating God's promise. I can claim God's marvelous promise in 1 John 1:9: "If we confess our sins, He is faithful and righteous to forgive us our sins and to cleanse us from all unrighteousness." "Confess" means to agree with God. "God, I was impatient." "God, my attitude was wrong." Whatever it is, I name the sin that breaks my relationship with Him. When I do, I know that He has heard and answered, according to 1 John 5:14, 15: "And this is the confidence which we have before Him, that, if we ask anything according to His will, He hears us. And if we know that He hears us in whatever we ask, we know that we have the requests which we have asked from Him." After I confess (or exhale) the sin in my life, I inhale, or by faith appropriate the fullness and control of the Holy Spirit in my life. As a result, I am able to continue in unbroken fellowship with God.

Sin is the only thing that can prevent the Holy Spirit from being in control once we have received Christ and the Holy Spirit has come to indwell us. That doesn't mean that we are not Christians; it simply means that our sins stand in the way of our relationship and fellowship with God.

I have tried to develop the habit of keeping "short accounts" with God. That is, the moment I'm aware of sin, I confess it. I have learned that as I walk closely with God, acts of disobedience become less frequent. The more I obey Him, the more He gives me the power of the Holy Spirit to resist the temptation the next time.

According to hundreds of thousands of surveys which we have taken, 95 percent of all Christians surveyed have indicated they do not understand the ministry of the Holy Spirit and as a result are living defeated lives. I believe that this is because they do not claim this promise of God or understand the concept of spiritual breathing and of being controlled by the Holy Spirit.

The story is told of a mature Christian who shared with a young man that he had not experienced an hour of defeat in fifty years. The young man asked, "Do you mean you have not sinned in fifty years?"

"No," he replied, "I did not say that. I said I have not experienced an hour of defeat in fifty years." He went on to explain that though on occasion he disobeyed God, he never allowed an hour to pass without confessing his sin and appropriating the power of the Holy Spirit.

Are you sure that you are filled with the Holy Spirit? If you aren't, wouldn't you like to be sure? Let me encourage you to recognize that being filled and controlled by the Holy Spirit is a matter of faith, of simply desiring to be filled and surrendering control of your life to Christ.

By faith, thank the Lord for filling you. If you want to be scripturally precise, you don't need to ask the Holy Spirit to fill you. Simply acknowledge that He lives in you and thank Him for filling you as He promised to do when you trust and obey Him.

You may wish to pray the following prayer:

Dear Father, I acknowledge that I have been in control of my life. I realize I have sinned against You. Thank You for forgiving my sins through Christ's death on the cross for me. I now invite Christ to again take control of the throne of my life. Fill me with the Holy Spirit as You *commanded* me to be filled and as You *promised* You would do if I asked You. As an expression of my faith, I now thank You for taking control of my life and for filling me as You promised. In Jesus' name. Amen.

Being rightly related to God assures a Christian woman that she has everything needed to handle her daily problems. God has given us that assurance through the power of the Holy Spirit and the many promises in the Bible. One promise which has been especially important to me is, "Cast all your anxieties upon Him, for He cares for you" (*see* Peter 5:7).

At a time when I was particularly concerned about a situation, Dr. Henrietta Mears said, "Vonette, you're so weighted down with all these problems, I want you to prayerfully identify each problem. Then visualize taking all of your problems and placing them in a big box, tying them tightly with a ribbon and giving them as a gift to God. Tie the box tight with ribbon so you can't get those things out. Now, visually hand the box to God and let loose."

Then Miss Mears said sternly, "Now that you've given your cares to God, stop stealing His property!"

Once a sin is confessed or an anxiety is cast upon the Lord, do not continue to worry about it.

I began to understand the real significance of this verse through an illustration given by Dr. Louis Evans, Sr. He related that several young children found a dead bird and decided to conduct a funeral to bury it. They made a casket out of a matchbox and lined it with cloth, while one of the boys whittled a little cross. During this procedure, another boy appointed himself the preacher. Then they sang songs and finally the bird was buried. Dr. Evans had amusingly observed this activity from his study window.

The next day the children, remembering the fun of the day before, dug up the bird to repeat the ceremony again. After the bird had been dug up and reburied several times, a noticeable odor came from the area. Deciding the bird needed to be buried once and for all, Dr. Evans went out to have one final funeral service with the children.

We need to bury our concerns and frustrations with finality, too. When we give them to God, they should remain buried. If we dig them up, they, too, have a terrible odor and can affect us and those around us.

There are always going to be situations in our daily lives which give us the opportunity to apply what we believe. No matter how challenging or exciting one's life may be, there is always the ordinary, whether it be emptying wastebaskets, preparing three meals a day for unappreciative teenagers, trying to communicate with an uncommunicative husband, or sitting in the same chair at the same desk and eating lunch with the same people in the same cafeteria. But it is because of these routine activities that it is especially important to know how to walk closely with the Lord. As I have trusted Him in the many different situations that confront me in a day, I find my frustrations and concerns, as well as the trying circumstances, can be dealt with immediately and effectively.

The more I rely upon the enabling power of the Holy Spirit, the greater becomes my understanding of the full and meaningful life—the abundant life—that Jesus promised.

# 6 Hardly an Accident

I love being a woman—a woman who is rightly related to God! It was God who specifically decided I was to be female. Some women claim their sex is a freak accident. But I have the assurance from the Bible that God made me the sex I am for His glory and purpose, just as He made Jeremiah the prophet the way he was for His special purpose: "I knew you before you were formed within your mother's womb; before you were born I sanctified you and appointed you as my spokesman to the world" (Jeremiah 1:5 LB).

David, the psalmist, also indicates that God is in control of our lives: ". . . Thou didst weave me in my mother's womb. . . . Thine eyes have seen my unformed substance; And in Thy book they were all written, The days that were ordained for me, When as yet there was not one of them" (Psalm 139:13, 16).

But even though God is in control of our lives, knowing how our days will be spent, He has also given us the free will to determine what we are going to do with the lives He has given us. As a result, there is no set role for women, no pattern given scripturally to which all women must conform. In the Bible, women were prophetesses (*see* Judges 4:4, 5; Exodus 15:20, 21; 2 Kings 22:14-20; Luke 2:36-38); they served as rulers (*see* 2 Kings 11:1-16; Acts 8:27); and they were outstanding businesswomen (*see* Proverbs 31:16; Acts 16:14; 1 Chronicles 7:24). God has not confined women, so why should we as Christians limit women in what they can do?

In whatever we choose to do, we will influence at least 160 people, according to information compiled by Dr. McFarland, educational consultant of General Motors. He says, "Every individual, no matter how insignificant he may be or in what remote area of the world he may live, influences at least 160 people in his lifetime."

But most of us, when we look at the world and the circumstances in which we live, think, *If the world is going to be influenced by me, it's an absolutely hopeless cause.* Because we know our personal inadequacies, defeats, and discouragements so well, we wonder how we could possibly be of help to anyone else.

Many of the prophets of the Old Testament and disciples in the New Testament felt much the same way. After God had called Moses to lead the people out of Israel into the Promised Land, Moses said, "Oh, Lord, I'm no more fit to do this than I was when You first called me forty years ago." In Exodus 4:14, we are told that God was displeased by Moses' response.

God is also displeased with our excuses. When God gives us an idea to do a task or the guidelines to perform it, we sometimes say, "Oh, let somebody else do it. I don't want to," or "I don't have any ability. I am not equal to the task."

It was obvious from the men God chose to do His work that He did not need their abilities. For example, when Joshua took over Moses' job to lead the Israelites to Canaan, God said, "Every place on which the sole of your foot treads, I have given it to you . . ." (Joshua 1:3). God had already given the land to Israel. All that He needed to accomplish the task was Joshua's availability, and all He needs of us today is our availability.

When God calls us to a task and we make ourselves available to Him, it is His responsibility to give us the ability to control the circumstances, to provide the finances, to do whatever is necessary to accomplish the task.

It's an exciting experience when God works through us to accomplish what He wants. I was particularly aware of this after my husband brought me to Arrowhead Springs to consider purchasing the former luxury hotel which had gone bankrupt four and a half years before. We looked at the 136 rooms in the hotel, the ten cottages, two large dormitories, and the other buildings on approximately eighteen hundred acres of land. Neither one of us knew anything about operating a hotel, and after looking at the buildings and the grounds, I thought the work would absolutely kill us.

But Bill was certain that God intended Arrowhead Springs to be the international headquarters for Campus Crusade for Christ. The staff had grown from only Bill and myself in October 1951 to almost two hundred people in 1962. Bill was sure that this facility would accelerate our ministry one hundred times. His prophecy has more than come true with a present staff of more than five thousand members serving Christ in eighty-five countries.

As we stood in the beautiful Wanih Room of the hotel, overlooking the San Bernardino valley, Bill said, "Honey, I have the assurance that God wants us to have Arrowhead Springs for this ministry, and we'll be in this place by fall."

Absolutely amazed, I replied, "Dear, you must be crazy! Even if we were able to purchase Arrowhead Springs by fall, we wouldn't want to move in until it was adequately refurbished."

Accompanying us were a professional builder and his wife, who was an interior decorator. After hearing my statement, the woman turned to Bill and in a light vein said, "Bill, I'm going to pray for you."

He quickly replied, "Don't pray for me. Pray for my wife." Well, we were in the building by fall. It was late fall, but fall nonetheless. It was amazing to see the way in which God provided not only the financing but also the ability and the people with expertise in needed areas to help operate Arrowhead Springs. Since 1962, hundreds of thousands of students, older adults, and pastors have been trained at Arrowhead Springs. God has honored availability and active faith.

Every woman wants to be used of God, unless she is satisfied with a mediocre existence or is unaware of the joy that comes from being available to Him. Most women, whether they express the desire or simply think about it in the quiet of their own hearts, want the world to be a better place because of their lives. But how can we make positive contributions?

First of all, we must begin where we are, and for the majority of us, that is in the home.

Today the home and family are facing a great crisis. The family, as we have traditionally known it, is threatened as never before. According to the *1976 World Almanac,* in 1974 there were more than four new divorces granted for every ten new marriages. The question of authority in the home, the substitution of material things for real love and unity, alcoholism, drugs, and the influence of the radical scene are making their marks on our home situations.

Yet the home is the most important institution in the whole world. It is even more important than the church because the home is the builder of the church. And it is more important than the nation because the home is the builder of a nation— all of society is affected by what goes on in the home. The enormous influence a woman has in her home offers quite a responsibility and an ideal place to begin saying, "God, I'm available to be used by You. Make me a better wife and mother —a better homemaker."

Whether or not home life includes a husband, or a husband and children, it is clear from Scripture that our first priority must be to love and obey God. Jesus told us that the greatest, or most important, of all the commandments is "You shall love the Lord your God with all your heart, and with all your soul, and with all your mind" (Matthew 22:37). Jesus also told us that we should seek God and His righteousness first, then all the other things we need will be added to us (*see* Matthew 6:33). He said that we prove we love Him when we keep His commandments (*see* John 14:21).

There is a very popular, romantic idea that God made one man and one woman just for each other. I choose to believe that. I'm sure that Bill Bright was made for me and I for him. But it is easy to imply, according to this thought, that the art of being happily married consists simply of finding the right person. However, I believe the art of staying happily married and having a happy home consists of being the women God wants us to be. This is why, among many other reasons, our first priority in our homes should be to love and obey our Lord and to be responsive to the leading of His Holy Spirit. He is the one who enables us to discover ourselves.

As wives, Scripture indicates that our second priority in our homes should be our husbands (*see* Ephesians 5:22-24). Because of the intimate and exclusive nature of the marriage relationship, God gives us a number of very important commands, which, if obeyed, will help to insure a happy and fulfilling relationship with our husbands. Even more important, as we obey God's Word, our influence in our husbands' lives will make them happier, more fulfilled individuals.

God tells Christian husbands and wives that they are to "be subject to one another" out of reverence for Christ (Ephesians 5:21), and following this admonition, wives are specifically told to "be subject" to their husbands (Ephesians 5:22). However, God's plan is obviously not one which includes the demeaning enslavement of women to their husbands. That is made quite plain through His instruction for mutual submission.

No organization, whether it be marriage or business, functions well without a head or someone to act as a final authority. It is also rare for a business partnership to work smoothly when all the leaders have equal authority. Consequently, in God's wisdom, He has arranged for the smooth functioning of a marriage by giving the husband final accountability for the decisions: "For the husband is the head of the wife, as Christ also is the head of the church . . ." (Ephesians 5:23).

In most marriages there is a good bit of compromise and concession, but no matter how your household is run, situations will undoubtedly arise when there will be a difference of opinion. As Ruth Graham, wife of Dr. Billy Graham, once said, "If two people agree on everything, one of them is unnecessary." Consequently, there must be a final authority to deal with the problem and make the ultimate decision.

Jeanne Hendricks, wife of Christian educator and psychologist Howard Hendricks, illustrates the problem from an experience she had with her mother during one afternoon of shopping. While they were going through the stores, they had to walk through many doorways. At each door they would waste time—hesitating, each politely insisting that the other go through first. After a few times of this she realized the necessity for having a final authority—for one of them to decide who was going to walk through the doors first. The same was true, she decided, concerning the many "doors" husbands and wives have to go through together. Someone must make the final decision.

By giving final authority to the husband, God protects the wife and family and makes the basic provision for the smooth functioning of marriage. Just as in the creation of the universe God provided order, so He continued that order in the family structure. As Paul affirms in 1 Corinthians 14:33, "God is not a God of confusion but of peace. . . ."

Another passage from God's Word, given for the benefit of wives, declares, "Wives, fit in with your husbands' plans . . ." (1 Peter 3:1 LB). Fitting into his plans is not always easy, but as you choose to do it and are available to let God work through you, you will be helping your husband and thus showing your love all the more. Obedience to God-given authority results in special blessing. The benefits include those given to the woman in Proverbs 31—her husband rises up to bless and praise her.

A friend, whose husband is a doctor, has applied this verse to her marriage, and as a result, this petite, feminine woman has entered into an activity she never imagined herself doing. Her husband loves to ride motorcycles because it offers him complete release from the pressures of his medical practice, and he wanted her to join him. So, in obedience to Scripture, she put aside her fear, overcame her natural reservation, and learned to ride. Soon afterward they took a several-hundred-mile-trip together on their motorcycles. Since then, they have taken many trips to visit their children at college. As a result of fitting into her husband's plans, this wife now declares that they are having the time of their lives, but it started because she was available to God and desired to please her husband.

In Ephesians 5:33, the Amplified Bible beautifully expresses further direction for wives: ". . . let the wife see that she respects and reverences her husband—that she notices him, regards him, honors him, prefers him, venerates and esteems him; and that she defers to him, praises him, and loves and admires him exceedingly."

Treating our husbands in the way this verse suggests would, among many other things, show them how precious they are to us. We also have God's promise that His word will not return void (see Isaiah 55:11). If our behavior is in accordance with His will and His Word, our marriages will be full and meaningful and our lives and relationships richly blessed as a result.

"You don't know my husband," you may say. But the Scripture doesn't say, "Love him if he is worthy"; Scripture says, "Love him!" Love him if he's an alcoholic, if he beats you, if he's unkind to the children, if he gambles away your money. Wives, you are commanded to love him—love him with God's kind of love expressed in 1 Corinthians 13. This kind of supernatural love is an expression of the will which we claim by faith. Christians are commanded to love without exception. This is a staggering thought until we realize that God does not command us to do something He doesn't enable us to do. Jesus told us to love others as He loved us (*see* John 15:12), and throughout the New Testament we see much Scripture that would indicate that the mark of the Christian should be love. Since we are commanded to love others we can claim God's promise that if we pray according to His will He will hear and answer (*see* 1 John 5:14, 15). God has an unending supply of love we can draw upon. This is what my husband calls loving by faith.

With children, a mother also has ample opportunity to pray, "God, I'm available. Use me, enable me to influence my children correctly." Because the mother is the cohesive factor in the family, she has many responsibilities. But if she only half-heartedly attends to the welfare of her husband and children, she leaves her family wide open to the threatening pressures of our day. A father may wander away and not be the man he should be as a father, but if the mother is stable, the children will not necessarily suffer. For when the mother is stable, the home can be kept together and her children can have the opportunity to grow up to be honorable and contributing citizens. But let the mother go astray and desert her family, and the result is usually catastrophic in the lives of the children. I've never seen it to be otherwise.

It is a mother's responsibility to make home a place the family enjoys and not just a shelter. In doing this, she should be available to listen to the children's problems, communicate goals, and teach responsibility.

In today's permissive society, all too often we offer children things rather than personal attention and love, for the giving of self takes real effort. But the mother who sacrifices her time to pick up her children immediately after school, or who is home when they return from school, finds it easier to communicate with them when they are excited about the events of the day than to try to pick up an hour or two later after their enthusiasm has worn down. Then the conversation many times becomes more of a question-and-answer type of communication, which isn't very satisfying to either children or parent.

In every home, family-directed activities are needed to give attention to the children. And who better than the mother can give thought and creativity to this activity. Intelligent, energetic youth are bored with nothing to do. If we as mothers do not help provide constructive activities, our children are going to find something to do on their own, and it may not be so constructive.

Doctor Harold J. Ockenga, president of Gordon-Conwell Theological Seminary, has said:

> The loosening of morals in many college communities, which has reached a new high, reflects a failure on the part of the older generation but presents a problem with which we have to deal. The problem has arisen from too many working women, too many broken homes, too many broken families, too much drinking, too much loose living, and too much pleasure seeking. Self-discipline and discipline of families are gone from American life.

God has given us specific instruction in how to rear our children. We are to tenderly discipline, train, and instruct them in the ways of the Lord (*see* Proverbs 13:24; 19:18; 22:6; 23:13; Ephesians 6:4).

My mother used to say, "When children are small they step on your toes, but when they are grown, they step on your heart." Personally, I'd rather they stepped on my toes. But throughout the twenty-two years of raising our sons, I've realized the necessity of trusting the Lord and of being available so that He could use me to help make them become the kind of men He wants them to be.

Without neglecting their families, many women desire to channel their abilities and time into activities away from home. According to *Commerce Today* magazine, today 46 percent of all women work. Labor Department statistics tell us that 38 million women who make up more than 47 percent of the total work force. Obviously, women find a need to work outside their homes, whether to express and develop themselves, to be involved in other people's lives, or to provide more material comforts and greater economic security.

From the biblical standpoint, the way is clearly open for the homemaker to use her time as she chooses outside her home. Women in the Bible played many different roles in life while still being faithful to their call as wives and mothers. As we learn from Proverbs 31, a woman can be a successful business-woman as well as a wife and mother.

Despite the number of women who work, many wives are perplexed about what they personally should do. I think there are several steps in determining God's direction for involvement away from home.

The first consideration is your motivation—why do you desire to work? The Christian woman's first concern should be, "How can I most honor and best serve the Lord Jesus Christ?" For many women, involvement outside of the home would expand their ministry many, many times. For others, a personal ministry would be enhanced by spending more time developing home relationships and giving greater attention to the family.

A person's motivation to become gainfully employed can also include her need to provide financial assistance for the family, help to pay for a house, put a husband through school, or provide the means for greater security later in life. However, no woman should sacrifice the welfare of her family to make extra money merely for luxuries. The trade-off is not worth the result.

With five children, our friends Nancy and Jack were struggling to support their family on his income. After a period of time, they realized he should return to college to finish his degree; however, to enable him to do so, Nancy had to take a full-time job. Without a skill and with the demands of five children, she realized it would be difficult to be employed. After

An
Easter
Remembrance

creatively considering her ability and availability, she began to work with crafts. Shortly afterward, the entire family became involved, and they organized a small business. With her children's help, Nancy has been so successful that Jack has decided to go on for his master's degree and will have a promising position waiting for him when he finishes his education.

Nancy's motivation was to fit into her husband's plans and help him fulfill his desires. His concern was to provide a better living for the family and to enable both of them to better serve Christ in whatever avenue God would lead.

While not desiring to be gainfully employed, Lois sought an opportunity to use her spare time and talent advantageously. She volunteered to make room decorations for an elementary classroom. The teacher soon realized that Lois was an outstanding artist and asked if she would teach the children for a portion of one day a week. Through this, Lois became involved with the Parent-Teacher Association and was able to participate in school-policy decisions. Later she became an officer in the city P.T.A. and then a representative at the state convention.

Because Lois had a desire to be involved outside her home and had one day a week available, she made the best use of her time by becoming involved with the school. As a result, she had many opportunities to express moral and spiritual values, share her faith, use her time to the best advantage, and satisfy her own need for self-expression, allowing her to influence not only her own child's life but also the lives of a roomful of children.

Women are liberated to choose what they wish to do, yet the woman seeking God's direction will find freedom by following the leading of the Holy Spirit in her life. For some, quitting their jobs or curtailing their activities away from home will be most honoring to Christ; however, for others, it may be to seek employment or to get involved in volunteer activities. Many would have us believe that women are to spend all of their time at home, never to be in the work force unless it is an absolute necessity. Others say it is imbecilic to merely try to maintain one's equilibrium at home. But because Christ is working in and through us, a Christian woman's life-style is revolutionary, and she does not have to be molded into either category.

Another consideration in determining God's direction for involvement away from home is your own desire. From the Bible we learn that God wants to give us our desires: "Delight yourself in the LORD; And He will give you the desires of your heart" (Psalms 37:4).

In many circumstances I have had to say, "Lord, if this desire isn't of You, take it away. If it is of You, keep it prominent in my thinking." When I'm assured it's from God, then I prayerfully ask for direction in how my desire can be fulfilled.

As I have waited for my prayers to be answered, I have found the answers come in God's perfect timing—not always in my timetable, but in His perfect time. God is faithful to all His promises.

Many times the sacrifice and adjustments which a woman must make to be involved outside her home test her commitment to those activities. In a Bible-study class I recently taught, a woman with two high-school-age children told me of her desire to return to college to finish the requirements for her degree.

Despite her family's enthusiasm for her undertaking, when it was time to leave for the 7:00 P.M. class, inevitably one of the children needed a ride somewhere or felt ill and needed her attention. Consequently, she either had to miss the class or make special arrangements to go. In addition, she found that it was difficult to get all of her family home for dinner early enough to clean the kitchen before she left.

The woman decided that she either had to ask the family to rise to the occasion and clean up the kitchen or face dirty dishes when she returned. She questioned whether it was really worth all the effort to have time for personal development. Of course, this problem can be solved only by the individual.

The fulfillment of desires does not usually come without some degree of sacrifice or inconvenience. This is why when a woman is certain of God's direction, she will have the motivation to continue in spite of the difficulties. Most importantly, when a woman is certain of God's direction, she will find the fulfillment she desires.

Another consideration which will affect a woman's involvement outside her home is her ability. If she has natural ability, training, or special expertise that would make her able to achieve or fit into a particular task outside her home, then channeling her self-expression is relatively easy. If not, it may be necessary to be creative. Many women justify boredom because they do not have any special skills or expertise. Yet often they have never seriously considered all the possibilities for broadening themselves.

For example, what are your interests? How much time do you have to devote to a project? Who could help you get involved? Can you learn a particular skill or how to accomplish a particular task?

The ages and needs of your children and your husband's desires are other primary considerations. I have learned from my friends' husbands, as well as my own husband, that their suggestions and observations can be extremely helpful. Our husbands know us well and can objectively look at our abilities, motivation, and desires and wisely counsel us on assuming additional responsibilities.

Being available to God is being responsive to the leading of the Holy Spirit. Through the Spirit, God leads us by His Word. Sometimes He speaks through circumstances or other persons or through impressions we are given. As we make ourselves available, we are simply saying to God that we will fit into His plan for us.

We can't possibly outgive God. As we make ourselves available to Him, He allows us to be far more fulfilled and to see greater results than we possibly could outside His will. God owes no man anything, yet His rewards are far more fulfilling and satisfying than any we could possibly imagine. To be available is not always easy, but there is no other way to achieve a more satisfying and victorious life.

God's plan leaves no room for freak accidents. He has created us as we are, with a free will to choose, a mind to create, and time to determine how we will invest our lives even in such a time as this.

# 7 Running the Circus

During one of my mother's visits, we were invited to luncheon at a friend's home. Mother was to be the honored guest, so we hurried madly to be on time. On the way I realized that I had forgotten a folder of material I needed that afternoon, but we didn't have time to go back.

After lunch I dashed to the beauty shop. As I sat under the hair dryer, images of the work in the folder that I should have been doing spoiled my concentration on the articles I was trying to read.

Leaving the shop slightly disgruntled, I planned to do my grocery shopping. As I walked in the supermarket door it occurred to me that I had used my last check at the beauty shop and was out of cash. I resigned myself to the inconvenience and loss of time and decided to get the car washed since I couldn't buy groceries. As I started to pay for the full tank of gas and car wash, I discovered I didn't have my credit card. The woman helping me was very gracious and suggested I use an old ticket with my credit-card number on it; however, the adjustment she had to make took a great deal of time and inconvenienced both of us.

On my way home I rebuked myself quite sternly: *Oh, if you'd just taken a few moments to think through this afternoon . . . if you'd just picked up your folder, everything would have been so much better.* Engrossed in my unwise use of time, I absent-mindedly took a wrong turn on the freeway which delayed my arrival home and inconvenienced me even further.

That was just one afternoon in my life, but such events can permeate a person's entire lifetime. Instead of disorganization, there is the alternative of time management. Basically, time management is thinking ahead, planning what you are going to do before you do it. It encompasses stewardship of your time, talent, and treasure—of all that God has given to you. Time management involves determining what you really want to accomplish and then putting those goals into your plans for a week, a year, and a lifetime.. Time management gives direction to the homemaker. It helps you see the importance of what you are doing because your activities are bringing you closer to achieving your long-term goals.

Many times people feel that a schedule is limiting. They don't want to be organized because they like to do what they want, when they want. Of course, this can be thought of as liberating. However, I have found that nothing has liberated me more than when I have planned ahead, claiming God's wisdom. If we don't plan ahead, when we come to the end of life having done "what comes naturally," we must be prepared to accept the fact that our lives may have counted for very little that is worthwhile.

It is important to remember, too, that time management is not designed to confine but to give the freedom to organize yourself to accomplish the things that you feel are important, worthwhile, and that contribute to making you the person you want to be. After all, if you aim at nothing, you are sure to hit it.

Of course, when there are many, many, interruptions in a person's life, such as meeting the needs of small children, then you have to plan more loosely. It is necessary to be less structured. However, it is especially important under these circumstances to know how you want to use your free time when you get it.

The parable of the talents (*see* Matthew 25) is a significant illustration of managing yourself. The story concerns a master, who, while planning a journey, entrusts a portion of his money to three servants. To one man he gives five talents, to another two, and to another one, each according to his ability. Upon his return, the master rewards the first and second servants because they have handled the money wisely and returned a profit to him. However, the master punishes the third servant because he hid his money and did not receive profit from it. The story teaches us that if we don't use our time or what God has given us to the very best advantage, we find even that which has been given to us is taken away.

In Proverbs 31:10-31 we see a picture of an organized woman with direction and goals for her life. She is a very productive woman who is satisfied with herself. Not only is she satisfied and fulfilled but her husband and her children delight in her also. Since we, too, want the best for our lives, we must seek the Lord and what He wants us to do.

In Psalms 37:23, we find, "The steps of a man are established by the LORD; And He delights in his way." Scripture also tells us, "I will instruct you and teach you in the way which you should go; I will counsel you with My eye upon you" (Psalm 32:8). As we look to Him, He promises to direct our steps.

A planned life is a part of God's plan, for among the fruit of the Spirit is self-control or management of yourself (*see* Galatians 5:23). If you fail to plan, you should plan to fail:

For which one of you, when he wants to build a tower, does not first sit down and calculate the cost, to see if he has enough to complete it? Otherwise, when he has laid a foundation, and is not able to finish, all who observe it begin to ridicule him, saying, "This man began to build and was not able to finish" (Luke 14:28-30).

Another encouragement to manage ourselves is found in Ephesians 5:15, 16: "Therefore be careful how you walk, not as unwise men, but as wise, making the most of your time. . . ."

Considering the passage carefully, let's focus on an unwise woman. This person does not take into account the opportunities that are given her, nor does she consider what she can do with what she has. Her haphazard outlook toward life finds her starting something but never finishing it, or making a job last longer than it should because she has no priorities to motivate her. There is a principle in management circles called Parkinson's Law, which states that a job expands in proportion to the amount of time allotted to it.

To illustrate, let's look at the project of breakfast dishes. If there is no hurry to get the dishes finished, the homemaker may decide to have a second cup of coffee and look at the paper after the family is out of the house. Then she decides to go out to the garden to see how the roses are doing. While outside, she chats with her neighbor across the back fence. The neighbor suggests she come in to see her new draperies, so she goes over to visit. By now it is almost noontime, her dishes are still not washed, and the beds have not been made. When the end of the day comes, nothing productive has been accomplished because she has not used her time well. As it goes on day after day after day, week after week, month after month, year after year . . . time defeats her and a feeling of guilt and a poor self-image result.

On a larger scale, we can find that a wrong assessment of priorities contributes to unwise planning. My generation has worked hard to provide material possessions for their children. The automatic household equipment and the material possessions offer us efficiency, comfort, and more leisure time. In our desire to provide well, many have offered their children cars long before they graduate from high school, they have purchased mountain homes or beach homes or even airplanes—all kinds of luxuries—only to find they have not really brought happiness to their children or to themselves.

The father has been so busy providing these things, and the mother has been so busy taking care of them, that many times the children have been ignored. Along with material "success," the pressures of keeping all of the material possessions going have brought discontent.

Couples are now experiencing tragedies and heartache they never before dreamed they would be facing. Husbands who are working for that degree of success and wives who are finding their satisfaction in careers often discover they have lost their children. Many of the young people who were and are a part of the hippie drug culture have come from just such homes.

Frequently a husband who works very long and hard hours to "provide the best for his family" finds that his whole family has turned against him because he hasn't given them his time and attention. It isn't the material possessions his family has desired of him—it is his companionship that they have wanted. So husbands and wives reach the end of their lives and see that their family members are all going in separate directions, and that as parents they have failed at the very things they had really hoped to accomplish.

The need for the establishment of priorities and time management becomes even more apparent as we realize that, as women, many times we go through transitional periods. Our lives may run smoothly for one, three, or five years, but the demands on us and our own needs often fluctuate with the ages of our children, our husbands' activities, or other things that affect our families, such as a move or a promotion.

When our two children were small and I was in a domestic routine, I felt that life had been far more exciting when I was teaching school or ministering with Campus Crusade full time on the campus. I began to feel that my life was not productive and I became more and more dissatisfied with my life.

In the middle of one night I awakened and felt the need to get up, move into another room so that I would not awaken Bill, and study my Bible. I opened it to the parable of the talents.

Recognizing that these men were given certain responsibilities, or talents, I began to consider what God had given me and what I was doing with it.

God had given me a husband. He had given me each of my children. At that time, we were sharing a home with Henrietta Mears, so He had also given me a relationship with her. He had given us a beautiful home near the UCLA campus, and He had given me an organization within which I could have a ministry.

On note cards I wrote down the things I felt God would have me do for each one of them. It was interesting that the first thing the Lord seemed to say was to stop nagging my husband. I was reminded that my husband belonged to the Lord. At that time I felt that Bill was giving far too much of himself to Campus Crusade as well as to his business. I was afraid he was working so hard that he would die before his fiftieth birthday. But it was as if God said, "He is My responsibility; I'll take care of him. You are to help, not hinder him in his ministry. Stop your nagging."

I felt impressed that instead of nagging him, I should consider what I could do to help him. Since he needed high energy, I decided to go to the health-food store and find out what high-energy supplements would be good for him. I also realized I could help by seeing that he did not have to give undue consideration to meeting his own physical needs, and there were many ways in which I could relieve him of small responsibilities.

During this time we lived in an established neighborhood where there were few children. Although our oldest child, Zac, was in kindergarten, I knew he needed to play with friends "at his house." Also, because of the traffic and the bigness of the yard, it was dangerous for Zac to play without supervision, but he needed that freedom. I felt impressed to make a point of bringing in children at certain times during the week and to fence in an area in the backyard where Zac could play unattended. Our youngest child, Brad, was spending too much time by himself, I felt, so we enrolled him in nursery school.

Miss Mears, I thought, needed encouragement; I tried to see that she had plenty of opportunity to entertain her guests. Then I began to consider how we could use the house to a greater degree as a part of our outreach to the students and people in the community.

Now our circumstances as well as my family's needs have changed; however, the principle remains clear and useful. I think it is wise to evaluate each year, perhaps every few months, what you are doing, how well you are accomplishing your goals, how satisfied you feel with what is happening in your life right at that moment. As I have become more involved and more organized in my time management, I find it is wise to review my yearly plan every few months just to see how I'm doing.

In setting lifetime goals, Allen Lakin, an expert on time management, has suggested that people ask themselves, "By the time I blow out the candles on my seventieth birthday cake, what do I want to have accomplished in life?" Stop and consider for a couple of minutes and write down what you want to have, or hope to be true, by the time you are at the end of your life. In addition to the priority of serving our Lord, there could be lots of fun things you want to do—such as travel, or some particular far-out accomplishment such as climbing the Matterhorn— besides the very purposeful activities. Whatever your desires are, the goal is to identify what would be fulfilling to you.

Second, consider what you want to accomplish within the next five years. How are you going to be working toward accomplishing these lifetime goals? Often I hear people say, "Oh, I would love to play the piano." Five years from now, will they still be saying, "Oh, I would love to play the piano," or "I would love to paint china"? If that is a lifetime priority, break it down until you know what part of that goal you are going to accomplish in the next five years. Abraham Lincoln once said, "People are always getting ready to live, not really living." Don't let that be said of you.

For the third step in setting goals, consider what you would like to have completed one year from now. Finally, if you were to die six months from today, what are the urgent things you would wish to have accomplished? Would you want the children's photograph album put together or the closets clean? Would you like to complete a book that you have wanted to write?

Thinking in terms of the urgent as well as the long-term goals, begin to work these into a daily schedule. A time-management plan developed by Campus Crusade staff members Steve Douglass and Bruce Cook is taught in a Conference on Church Management. Bruce's wife, Donna, and I adapted this into a homemaker's personal-development plan, fitting into seven basic categories: spiritual, physical, mental, social, recreational, domestic, and financial. These areas can be used as guidelines for determining lifetime as well as short-range goals. For example: What is your lifetime goal spiritually? What is your lifetime goal mentally? Socially? And so on until you break your whole life down into workable areas.

In applying your year's goals to your schedule, I recommend that you concentrate on three of the seven categories that are priorities, and work with them until you experience success. Then move to your other categories.

Let me illustrate with my goal in the area of the physical. One of my lifetime goals is to feel good and to be physically as well as spiritually fit. My yearly goal is to develop a skill and to firm up my muscle tone. I decided that I would learn to play tennis and use a roller machine. Then I decided to fit these activities into my daily schedule by using the roller five minutes in the morning every day and playing tennis one hour a week on Thursday morning.

For years, I had been one of those persons who made lists of things that needed to be done: the laundry, the shopping, the baking, the planning, the music lessons, the dinner parties, the telephone calls—all kinds of things. As I completed tasks, I checked them off. My piece of paper could last for a day, a week, or a month. But by continually adding to the list, it wasn't long before my things-to-do were lost in all the markings. I have found that looking at one week at a time is an effective alternative. One of the rewards of a weekly schedule is to see how much free time I really do have. A long list worked into a week doesn't look so gigantic.

Some of us are more organized than others. Some of us like to work in a more structured framework than others. Adapt this to whatever your personal needs may be. You have to allow yourself lots of free time, especially when your children are small. If you are a person who receives many telephone calls, you must allow time to talk on the telephone. If there are people or situations that are constantly interrupting you, you have to schedule time for interruptions. If you are a highly regimented person and find your schedule is very organized, then your activities will be easier to schedule.

There are certain cautions to be aware of in scheduling. Don't try to emulate other people, but do what God wants you to do. When you are accomplishing what He has asked of you, you are highly motivated and you find that you have time for what He wants you to accomplish, not necessarily what everybody else wants you to. Recognize that God has made you a very unique individual. He has given you certain talents and capabilities.

Doctor Brandt compares a person's management of the activities in his life with running a circus. He says that some of us are able to run a one-ring circus. Then there are people who can manage a three-ring circus smoothly. If we can operate only a one-ring circus, keeping up our home, children, and husband while maintaining our equilibrium under pressure, that is all we should try to do. If a person can keep three rings going in the same way, then operate three rings. If you can do ten, then joyfully go about running those ten rings. But we need to be realistic with ourselves in terms of what we can personally accomplish. The person who can do more should not insist that others accomplish what she can, nor should the person who does less feel unfulfilled because she cannot do more.

Perhaps another pitfall could be best described as "Everybody get out of my way, here I come with my schedule." Being available to your family is part of time management, yet it is sometimes impossible to plan. So I caution you not to overplan; allow yourself time for the unexpected so that your schedule doesn't "run you" but you "run it."

A planned, Spirit-controlled life results in having the satisfaction of knowing that you're doing what you want to do and are living a fulfilled, meaningful life. It means choosing several things that you really enjoy doing and accounting for them in your schedule. It includes doing the humdrum variety of things which have to be done—and all of us have those projects—with more enthusiasm. You will find that those projects go much faster, are much easier, and in the end are more productive because you know that God wants you to do them. That helps you to desire to complete these goals. It is through the planned life that we find ourselves developing into the persons whom we want to be and whom God wants us to be.

# 8  Living a New Life

The first time I received a letter from Linda, she asked for my suggestions for helping high-school students improve the moral fiber of their community. She was a teacher and worked closely with the teenagers. After that, Linda wrote regularly to tell me about her work and the exciting opportunities she had to see many students come to know Christ.

After hearing from Linda for three years, I learned she had volunteered to care for the children during a Campus Crusade Staff Training, and I eagerly anticipated meeting her. After talking with Linda and arranging a time for us to meet, a friend said, "Linda doesn't think you'll like her after you see her." I realized from her comment that Linda had a physical handicap or deformity.

Later that week we were introduced. As she talked, she anchored her elbow in one hand to hold her chin steady as she tried to speak coherently. It was a joyful experience for both of us as we talked briefly. Then, as she turned to leave, I recognized the spastic condition of her frail body. Seldom have I been more moved than I was after meeting Linda.

What gave this woman the purpose and radiance she obviously experienced? What motivated her to strive for fulfillment and accomplishment? I knew that Linda would answer those questions without hesitation: Jesus Christ had given her real life.

Can Jesus Christ really affect the way in which Linda as well as others live their daily lives? Should there be any noticeable difference between the person who believes in Christ and the one who doesn't?

The Bible indicates that knowing Christ is the most exciting adventure the human mind can comprehend. But to some people, the image of the Christian is entirely contrary to that. They imagine the Christian woman to be characterized by drab, unattractive attire, one who has no joy and lives a self-sacrificing life. Of course, that image has little appeal for the progressive woman of today.

Others look at the professing Christian who attends church on Sunday but gives little evidence of religious convictions during the week. Her life-style and actions are pretty much the same as the non-Christian. So why add the burden of going to church?

But do these two impressions really epitomize the Christian? They don't to me, and they don't according to the Bible. I rejected that image long ago and determined in my own life to turn from that which was just form and ritual.

Like many others, I decided I wanted to live a quality of life that would enable me to live above the circumstances, to allow me to keep my cool when turmoil was all about me, and to have purpose and direction to life.

J. B. Phillips, in his preface to *Letters to Young Churches,* makes a unique observation about Christians:

> The great difference between present-day Christianity and that of [first century Christians] is that to us it is primarily a

performance, to them it was a real experience. We are apt to reduce the Christian religion to a code, or at best a rule of heart and life. To these men it is quite plainly the invasion of their lives by a new quality of life altogether. They do not hesitate to describe this as Christ "living in" them.

*If this life-style was true of the followers of Jesus two thousand years ago,* I asked myself, *can't it also apply to His followers today?*

The Christian life-style is not one of legalistic do's and don'ts, but one which is positive, attractive, and joyful. The Bible offers such a life-style through Jesus Christ.

The Bible clearly defines the qualities which would cause individuals to take notice of the life of a committed Christian and seek him out of the crowd. In Galatians 5:22, 23 we read, "When the Holy Spirit controls our lives he will produce this kind of fruit in us: love, joy, peace, patience, kindness, goodness, faithfulness, gentleness and self-control . . ." (LB).

A life-style completely different from the majority of us see or experience today is explained in Colossians 3. This passage points out more than twenty-three different aspects of the person controlled by the Holy Spirit.

It begins by making some rather extraordinary statements:

. . . set your sights on the rich treasures and joys of heaven where he sits beside God. . . . Let heaven fill your thoughts; don't spend your time worrying about things down here. You should have as little desire for this world as a dead person does . . . don't worship the good things of life, for that is idolatry (Colossians 3:1-5 LB).

What do words such as these really mean? One Sunday afternoon, after about two years of marriage, Bill and I came to an understanding. When Bill and I were married, his friends became my friends. Every place we went, he was very considerate and introduced me to people, but often I would find that he was involved in private conversations, projects, or committee meetings which did not concern me at all. I often spent long hours just waiting for him to finish his business.

One Sunday morning after church, a couple who always sought Bill's company asked to speak to him privately. They were very cordial and polite to me, but I felt ignored as they left me and went to another room. After one hour had passed into two, and two into three, Bill finally appeared. He was apologetic but I felt so rejected and unable to contribute that I could only respond with tears. Although Bill was very loving, it took me a little time to regain my composure.

That afternoon, after finishing dinner, Bill suggested that we prayerfully consider and then list on paper what we personally desired and wanted to accomplish in our lifetime. Highly motivated to set my goals and work toward mutual goals that would help us avoid incidents such as the one earlier in the day, I left the room.

Several hours later we began to compare lists. Both of us began with the desire to have the Holy Spirit guide us and to have our lives, separately and together, bring honor and glory to God. Bill went on to express the hope that his personal ministry would help change the world. Then every item following those two concerned God's direction in his personal life and ministry.

My list included two to four children and a house modest enough to entertain a person from skid row but comfortable enough to entertain the president of the United States. I thought we needed at least two automobiles—I suggested mine be a blue Ford sports car. It had occurred to me that since we were listing what we wanted we might as well be specific.

Although my list included immediate material concerns, the opportunity to consider what I really wanted and what God had for me was a very significant time. For it was from our concern for the future that I began to really set my thoughts on the riches, treasures, and joys of heaven. After realizing God's desires for us, it was as if the struggle for material possessions, prestige, and honor were all cast aside. That day we signed a contract with the Lord, in which we relinquished all claim to our lives. A short time later, God gave the vision for Campus Crusade for Christ. It is doubtful that God would have trusted us with this ministry had we not first made a full surrender of our lives to Christ.

Considering a few other admonitions in Colossians 3, we find: "Away then with sinful, earthly things; deaden the evil desires lurking within you; have nothing to do with sexual sin, impurity, lust and shameful desires . . ." (verse 5 LB).

It is almost impossible today to escape the influence of sexual lusts, violence, and drugs. Among the greatest contributors to increased immortality are television programs. Because I don't watch TV very often, every time I do, I am amazed at the increased use of violence, profanity, and emphasis on sex. What people were once concerned about and tried to remove from the viewing public now seems to be taken as a matter of course.

As the Bible is being attacked and ignored, we hear individuals in the public eye voicing some very liberal opinions which carry a great deal of influence. A famous woman doctor, who is a regular columnist in one of the popular women's magazines, now proclaims the practicality of trial marriages. A starlet whom many have loved and admired outspokenly discusses her practice of living with a person before marriage. Opinions such as these are affecting our entire society, but according to the authority of the Bible, they are completely wrong. The Bible tells us sex is beautiful in the bonds of marriage. However, lustful desires and unchastity are sin.

In Colossians 3 we find another admonition to live a new life: ". . . cast off and throw away all these rotten garments of anger, hatred, cursing, and dirty language" (verse 8 LB).

As I have had the opportunity to travel, I have become increasingly aware of the way in which the moral tone of our nation is changing. While traveling by plane from Alabama to

Georgia, an attractive young woman was seated beside me. As we talked, every three or four words in her conversation were profane. I had never heard a man utter some of the words she used. It used to be when you heard a person using this kind of language you found the person to be morally loose and coarse looking. Yet, this woman was intelligent and attractive.

Some religious leaders, whose theology does not embrace the authority of the Scriptures and the sovereignty and holiness of God, are often irreverent in using profanity in everyday speech. Recently, I had the opportunity to be part of a panel interviewing individual candidates for the presidency concerning their religious viewpoints. There were a number of panelists, and they represented various facets of the Christian community. During the three-day session, I noted that it was the clergymen such as I described, not the politicians who were unreserved in their use of profanity.

In contrast, Norman Cousins, in his book *In God We Trust,* tells us that during the revolutionary war, it had come to General Washington's attention that the enlisted men were using profanity. From his orders, we learn:

> The General most earnestly requires, and expects, a due observance of those articles of war, established for the government of the army which forbid profane cursing, swearing and drunkenness; and in like manner requires and expects, of all officers, and soldiers, not engaged on actual duty, a punctual attendance on divine service, to implore the blessings of heaven upon the means used for our safety and defence.

On another occasion, he wrote to tell his officers to deal with the despicable practice of profanity among the soldiers: ". . . we can have little hopes of the blessing of Heaven . . . if we insult it by our impiety. . . ."

If we applied these standards to our daily lives, society would be totally different. Just consider the difference a few other suggestions in this passage would make in your surroundings—if people did not tell lies, were tenderhearted, merciful and kind, didn't worry about making a good impression, were ready to suffer quietly and patiently, were gentle and ready to forgive, never held grudges, and were always thankful.

Colossians 3:15, 16 continues to point out:

> Let the peace of heart which comes from Christ be always present in your hearts and lives. . . . Remember what Christ taught and let his words enrich your lives and make you wise; teach them to each other and sing them out in psalms and hymns and spiritual songs, singing to the Lord with thankful hearts. LB

When our oldest son was in high school, occasionally he would come home from school and say, "Mother, how do you really know the Christian position is right?" As I would answer his arguments, there was one point that made a lasting impression when others seemed to fail. I would encourage him to look at the life-style of the true follower of Christ and consider how attractive it is. Then I would ask him to consider the non-Christian, and the qualities which were appealing in that life-style. He would then come to his own conclusion that the imitation of the life of Christ was the most appealing way to live.

Every true believer in Christ desires to follow these instructions from God's Word; however, the practice of these truths is often neglected because Christians do not know what the Word of God has to say. Without a knowledge and understanding of the Bible, it is easy to let the philosophies of men cloud the purity and wisdom of God's Word. Without the Bible as the measure of righteousness, it is easy to compromise our position or accept the words of others to determine our action or philosophy and, in turn, our own life-style. Christians are warned, "See to it that no one takes you captive through philosophy and empty deception, according to the tradition of men, according to the elementary principles of the world, rather than according to Christ" (Colossians 2:8).

The Apostle Paul said, "The things you have learned and received and heard and seen in me, practice these things . . ." (Philippians 4:9). When he wrote this, the people of Ephesus were facing many of the problems which confront us today. Yet, because he had clear direction for his own life from God, he knew he could challenge others to follow him.

Henrietta Mears had that same confidence, and her display of the Colossians 3 qualities in her life was what attracted me to her. As director of Christian Education at Hollywood Presbyterian Church, she had been very influential in helping to teach Bill about the Christian life. I had heard much about her, but I didn't know until later that she had been praying for me for a number of years. Miss Mears was very interested in Bill's future as a Christian leader, and she was afraid he was engaged to the wrong girl. So when we did meet, she took a great interest in me.

Physically, Henrietta Mears wasn't the most beautiful person I'd ever met. She was large boned and stocky and had dramatic features accented by thick-lensed glasses. Yet, if anyone should ask me, "Who is the most beautiful person you have ever known?" Henrietta Mears would be at the top of my list. Miss Mears had that inner quality which caused all who knew her to forget about her appearance. She was vibrant, alert, and adamant that knowing Christ was the most exciting adventure a person could ever experience.

After sharing our Bel Air home with Miss Mears for ten years, I learned that love was the quality she longed for most in her life. All who knew her would probably agree that she was the most loving person they'd ever known. However, she often shared that she hadn't always been that way but that God was continually building that quality into her.

I once saw her at the Hollywood Christian group when a young actress came to a meeting wearing too much makeup and too few clothes, and acted in an artificial manner. When others were critical, Miss Mears's sincere compliments of "Oh, isn't she darling," and "Oh, she's so sweet," did not go unnoticed. There was no artificiality in what she was saying. She genuinely saw the loveliness in every person, and she clearly understood God's love for man and believed that when a person embraced the Lord Jesus, he became an instrument of His love to the rest of the world.

As Miss Mears expressed her love to others, she caused all those who knew her to strive and usually to attain the highest achievement she thought possible of them. As a result of her encouragement, more than four hundred men are in the pulpit today, and additional men and women are on the mission field of the world plus the thousands of families who have established Christian homes as a result of her teaching.

Miss Mears had inner beauty because love shone through her life. But she readily confessed that she was the person she was because Jesus Christ had changed her.

That same positive alteration and radiant life-style is available to every Christian, and that life-style is the most exciting and attractive one I have ever heard about or seen in practice. It causes people to take notice. This radiance, which cannot be hidden, can be ours as we seek to trust and obey the Lord. It is a goal worth striving for. As Miss Mears would say, "Who would want anything but the best?"

# 9  A Strong Relationship

Christianity is a living relationship with the Person Jesus Christ. However, as in any relationship which has meaning, it must be worked at. As we are available to talk to, listen to, and do things for those we love, so must we spend time in the same manner getting to know Jesus Christ.

The most important source of information about Christ is the Bible. Consequently, it is necessary to study Scripture to know what it has to say. When we experience spiritual birth, it is extremely important that we have spiritual nourishment, just as in the first few hours after a baby is born he's fed with sugar and water. Then he moves on to a formula, and later, orange juice is added to his diet and then pablum.

So should it be with us as spiritual babies. After we first become Christians, we should begin to study His Word and act upon what we know. Just as babies are not concerned with what they can't eat but concentrate on what they can, so should new Christians concentrate on what they understand in the Word of God.

Tragically, there are many people who remain spiritual babies though they have been Christians long enough to be quite mature in their spiritual walk. A person who does not spend time alone with the Lord or time with other believers limits himself. He cannot know the rewards of a spiritually productive or abundant life as the person who spends more time with the Lord can.

I have known individuals who received Christ and began their spiritual walk on the same day. They got into the Word of God and began to apply spiritual truth to their lives and really "took off" as Christians. Others were slow, for they gave Bible study a low priority in their lives and consequently did not learn how to apply spiritual truths.

Scripture is relevant to every phase of our lives. I believe that one of the great needs of this hour is for us to know what the Bible has to say. Today, when no authority seems to rule our conduct, we need to get back to God's textbook for man.

God's Word speaks explicitly about topics ranging from our personal relationships to decisions in court. For instance, a friend of mine who operated her own business was taken to court and sued. Her lawyer assured her that the individual who was suing didn't have a case, but my friend lost. After the trial, one of the jurors came up to her to say she was sorry the decision had to be made against my friend. The juror said, "We knew you weren't guilty, but we also knew that you could afford to pay this penalty. Since there was financial need on the part of the other person, we decided in his favor." In executing justice, an understanding of the Word of God would have led the jurors to render a different decision.

In Exodus 23:3 we have clear instruction: "Nor shall you be partial to a poor man in his dispute." This would, of course, apply to the rich man as well.

A schoolteacher tells of a problem she faced in her classroom. A little boy had lost twenty-five cents and was quite distressed over his loss. Trying to comfort him, she instructed the

class to look for the quarter. After the children had been looking for a while, she thought, *Surely someone should have found
it by now*. When she inquired, one little boy spoke up and said
he had found the quarter. The teacher suggested he return it,
but the little boy said, "I will not. He lost it and I found it. So
the quarter is mine." She then found she could not exert any
real pressure to cause the young man to give it back to the boy
who had lost it.

The teacher left the classroom bewildered about what to do.
Obviously, according to the value system of the class, the response aptly expressed was, "Tough luck for the guy who
loses it."

In the Bible we see a different set of values. We are told that
that which is lost is to be returned to the owner, even if the
owner is your enemy. (*See* Exodus 23:4.)

Only as we know God's Word can we apply it to our lives,
and learning takes time and attention. Hebrews 4:12 tells us,
"The word of God is living and active and sharper than any
two-edged sword, and piercing as far as the division of soul
and spirit, of both joints and marrow, and able to judge the
thoughts and intentions of the heart." God's Word is strength-
ening. It brings peace to our hearts and gives direction to our
lives. Decisions which are made in the light of God's Word
are stable and show wisdom.

In 2 Chronicles 34, the story of Josiah and the impact the
Word of God had on him and on the nation of Israel is recorded.
After Josiah became king, he sought to know about Jehovah,
the God his grandfather David worshiped. After learning about
Him, Josiah embraced the God of Israel as his God and began
to tear down all the pagan temples and rebuild the Temple of
the Lord. In the Temple's reconstruction, the original scroll of
Moses was discovered and taken to Josiah. As Josiah read the
Scriptures, he began to understand that God's judgment would
be upon the people of Israel because they had disobeyed and
dishonored Him by worshiping idols and forsaking Him.

Josiah took the Scripture to Huldah, the prophetess, and she told him if he humbled himself before the Lord, interceding for his people, God would hear. Josiah called the people of Judah and the inhabitants of Jerusalem together and read them the Word of God. He then publicly declared that he would follow Jehovah and asked the others in the nation to do so, too. Because of their actions, God spared Israel during Josiah's lifetime.

Just as Josiah realized the importance of knowing what the Word of God had to say and then following it, so we must realize there are ramifications for us even today if we do not know and obey Him.

As we read the Bible, we find explicit direction in many matters which concern us. For instance, we learn what kind of husband a man is to be, the kind of wife a woman is to be, how to discipline and rear children, how to handle our relationships with other people. If we neglect the Bible, we cannot expect to benefit from the wisdom and direction which results from learning what God has to say.

Any time my husband and I have an important decision to make and the direction is not clear, we always seek the answer from Scripture. There was a time when we desired to have a third child. We had voiced this to some friends, and one day when Bill was away, I received a telephone call that someone wished to place a baby girl in our home for adoption. Already having two boys, I thought this was an absolute answer to prayer.

Bill was enroute home from a trip and I could hardly wait to tell him. I was certain that he would be excited because we had talked about having a little girl, but when I did get to tell him he completely surprised me by not immediately saying yes.

For hours we discussed the pros and cons of taking a new baby into our home. After consideration it seemed wisest not to take her, but I was emotionally involved and wanted to have a little girl. As we went to bed that night, I prayed that if God wanted us to adopt her, He would confirm it in my heart. But if we were not to have her, I asked to know from His Word that this was definitely His plan for us.

Within a few days, a staff member came to visit. Our guest had just purchased an Amplified Old Testament and enthusiastically read Proverbs 31 to me. As I listened, one verse (v. 16) caught my attention: "She considers a new field before she buys or accepts it—expanding prudently [and not courting neglect of her present duties by assuming others]. With her savings [of time and strength] she plants fruitful vines in her vineyard."

Suddenly I realized that I had all I could handle with the family God had given me and the increasing responsibilities of an expanding ministry. This verse confirmed to me the decision we should make, and as soon as God confirmed that fact, it took all my intense emotion of wanting a daughter away.

If you find that studying the Bible is uninteresting and that it is difficult to arrange time to do it, I understand. As a new Christian, I had to concentrate on finding time to read my Bible, and then discipline myself to do it.. But today, reading the Scripture is an absolute necessity to me, and I can't function well without prolonged times of Bible study and Bible reading. When my children were small, reading even a verse or two would sustain me through times of weariness. But today, with the special pressures of decisions and administrative responsibilities, that time in God's Word is vital in sensing His direction and guidance.

Because the reading of the Bible can be an overwhelming experience for many, with its histories, lineages, and strange names, let me give you some suggestions to begin. The Gospel of John is a good place to start your reading. I have found it helpful to underline all the verses that admonish us to believe and emphasize what we are to believe.

After studying the Book of John, you may wish to study the Books of Acts and Romans. Acts is a particularly important book because it tells of the early church, its leaders, and God's miracles. The Book of Romans explains what man is like without God, his need for a Savior, why it was necessary that Jesus Christ come, and the difference between a life governed by self and a life governed by the Holy Spirit.

When you've finished, read the New Testament through as quickly as possible. It can be read in about twenty-five hours. Read it two or three times before you go on to the Old Testament, and then read the Old Testament as quickly as possible.

To learn more about the Bible, you may want to consider purchasing a study book. You can work on your own or attend a Bible-study group. However, nothing can take the place of your personal reading and study. You need time alone to communicate with God. Try to spend time daily with the Lord, even if it's just five to fifteen minutes. As you mature in your walk, you will want to spend an hour or more reading and studying God's Word.

God speaks to us through His Word, but to cultivate this relationship we should learn to talk with Him. We communicate with God through prayer; however, the prayers of many people never go much beyond "Now I lay me down to sleep." Many people pray only in emergencies. Others find it boring, so they don't pray at all, while still others neglect prayer because they don't feel worthy. For many, it remains a relatively unknown experience.

Yet Jesus found it necessary to pray; He taught His disciples how to pray. Through history, we find those who have been outstanding in the cause of Christ are those who have prayed. The Scripture admonishes us to pray without ceasing (*see* 1 Thessalonians 5:17), which means talk to God hundreds of times a day. We are told there is nothing too small for His attention or too great for Him to accomplish.

The importance of prayer is recorded in many verses. In Jeremiah 33:3 God promises us that when we call to Him, He will show us great and mighty things we do not know. James 4:2 tells us that we have not because we ask not. Matthew 7:7

says, "Ask, and it shall be given to you; seek, and you shall find; knock, and it shall be opened to you." In John 16:24, Jesus makes this statement: "Until now you have asked for nothing in My name; ask, and you will receive, that your joy may be made full." The Bible places a very strong emphasis on prayer.

The basic reason people do not pray is that they do not know how to pray. Often when they do pray they don't see answers to prayer. Those who pray must first know that to receive answers they must be rightly related to God. They must belong to Christ (*see* 1 Timothy 2:5).

If I'm walking down the street and a little boy comes to me and says, "Will you please give me a nickel?" even though I've never seen him before, I will probably give him the nickel.

But when my own child says, "Mommy, give me a nickel," I usually know whether he needs it. If he does, I'm obligated as his parent to provide for that need, and even if he doesn't need it, I'll probably give it to him because he asked me, unless he would be harmed by my giving him the nickel.

With the first child, I have the choice; but with my own child, I'm obligated to provide for his needs. Also, because I love him, I will try to please him by giving him what he likes if it is for his best interest.

So it is in our relationship with God. When we receive Christ, we become children of God. Because of our new position, God promises to provide for our needs. But when we have not received Christ as our personal Savior, He is under no obligation to answer our prayers.

Another prerequisite to receiving answers from prayer is to have a clean heart: "If I regard iniquity in my heart, the Lord will not hear me" (Psalms 66:18 KJV). In other words, God will not listen to us if we have not confessed our sin. However, God clearly explains, "If we confess our sins, He is faithful and righteous [just] to forgive us our sins and to cleanse us from all unrighteousness" (1 John 1:9).

The third prerequisite to answered prayer is having a forgiving heart: "And whenever you stand praying, forgive, if you have anything against anyone; so that your Father also who is in heaven may forgive you your transgressions" (Mark 11:25). Many times I have heard someone say, "Oh, you can't expect me to forgive him. I could never forget what he did to me." Yet God expects us to forgive others so that we can receive His forgiveness and He can answer our prayers.

Those who pray must do so in faith; believing is a prerequisite for answered prayer.

In addition to these basic principles in praying, there are a few key words which will also enable us to pray confidently. First is the word *abide* as found in John 15:7. This verse is important to prayer; I've learned to call it the combination to heaven.

Imagine a bank safe with a gigantic door and a large combination lock on the front. This safe contains the treasures of heaven, God's safe of answers to prayer. But to open the door you have to apply the combination: "If you abide in Me," and turn the big wheel until it clicks, "and My words abide in you," we turn it in the opposite direction until it clicks, "ask whatever you wish," and again turn the combination wheel until it clicks, "and it shall be done for you." Now just take hold of the gigantic handle and open the door. Inside the safe are all of God's good things which are available to us if we simply apply that combination.

By His example and teaching, Jesus encourages us to ask God for specific requests—those which have to do with our needs, our relationships, or anything that concerns us.

God delights in listening to us express our desires to Him. Prayers do not have to be long, nor does a person need to be superspiritual to talk to God. He simply desires that we come to Him with clean hearts and pure motives.

It is beneficial to keep a prayer list where you record the request, the day requested, and the date answered. This may help to increase your faith as you specifically see the ways in which God is answering your prayers.

It is not necessary to be in any special position to pray. I find some of my greatest times of communication with the Lord are when I'm working with my hands and my mind is free to concentrate on talking to Christ. When I'm washing dishes, preparing meals, driving, or going about other daily tasks, I talk to Him about everything.

One of the most unusual answers to prayer I've had that has caused me to trust God for little things as well as big ones concerns a little butterfly pin. One afternoon as I was dressing for a speaking engagement, I put on a new dress and realized I needed a piece of jewelry to go with it. While searching through my jewelry box, I came across a silver butterfly. Because the dress was black and trimmed with gold, it occurred to me how outstanding a gold butterfly pin would be. It had long since been my habit to pray about everything, so I said, "Lord, help me find a gold butterfly to go with this dress." A butterfly is one of my favorite symbols because it often gives an opportunity to talk about new life in Christ. Just as the butterfly depicts the transformation of the once ugly worm into a beautiful creature, so we become new when we receive Christ: "If any man is in Christ, he is a new creature; the old things passed away; behold, new things have come" (2 Corinthians 5:17).

Since I didn't have an appropriate piece of jewelry to wear, I put on a colorful scarf with the dress and went to my engagement. Later that evening, a friend approached me with a beautiful emerald-green velvet box. She said, "Vonette, my husband and I have purchased something for you."

When I opened it, there was the most exquisite piece of jewelry I'd ever seen. It was a gold jeweled butterfly.

No one could have known I'd asked for a butterfly. I had told no one and it had only been a few hours since I'd said anything to the Lord about it. Yet God answered "exceeding abundantly" above what I could ask or think, as is promised in Ephesians 3:20. I had asked for only a gold butterfly. This one had little rubies, sapphires, emeralds, and even two little diamonds, all individually set. From that gorgeous pin I learned a great spiritual lesson. If God is interested enough to provide a butterfly pin, He is more concerned with providing the large things we ask for, especially the spiritual needs of others.

I've learned to pray about everything. When unexpected guests come and I don't know what to serve, I'll pray, "Lord, show me what to do." Or when I'm baking and I don't have an ingredient, I'll pray God will show me what I can substitute. This prayer was especially necessary at a dinner party when I ran out of sauce that needed to stand for twenty-four hours. As I prayed, God gave me a creative mind. Instead of the fresh-tomato base, with which I originally started, I duplicated the taste with canned goods and spices I had in my pantry. Just as God gave me the answer in that situation, He gives each of us the ability to think creatively in the times we need it. From my own experience, as well as that of others, I've learned that God becomes a greater reality as we see how He answers prayers.

The power of prayer is so great that out of concern for our nation God has raised up a united prayer effort. The Great Commission Prayer Crusade, a ministry of Campus Crusade for Christ, was born to give women throughout the nation a united opportunity to influence moral and spiritual values and bring pressing needs to God in prayer. This ministry, which I have the privilege of directing, has in excess of twenty-five thousand active participants throughout the nation. These people receive a monthly mailing that alerts them to problems about which they can pray.

Since the beginning of this ministry four years ago, we have seen many nation-changing and personal answers to prayer. For instance, a teenage girl in one city was kidnapped and given up for dead after three weeks. As a result of united specific prayer in that city she was returned well, unharmed, and un-molested.

In December 1975 it was announced that the last Vietnamese refugee camp was closed as the last of the refugees found sponsors. Of the 131,000 refugees, over 80,000 found sponsors through church-related groups. Thousands had faithfully prayed for their physical and spiritual needs.

Also in December 1975, Atlanta officials reported that the crime rate was down 25 percent. The Christians believe it was because of a massive saturation campaign to share the message of Christ in every home. Police also claim credit for the reduction, but it is interesting to note that the change immediately followed AGAPE Atlanta, now known as "Here's Life, America." Praise God for the effect of both the Gospel and a good police force (*see* Romans 13:1-4).

(If you are interested in being a part of this prayer movement, write the Great Commission Prayer Crusade at Arrowhead Springs, San Bernardino, California 92414.)

Another consideration in the development of our relationship with God is obedience. It is hard to obey someone you do not know, nor even desire to. For this reason, it is important that every Christian understand who God is. As we read the Scriptures, it is good to look for the character, the capability, and the promises of God. As we study, we recognize that God is worthy of the trust we have placed in Him because He is loving, sovereign, omnipotent, holy, merciful, compassionate, faithful, and full of loving-kindness, as well as possessing many other characteristics.

A life of obedience is not a life of following a list of do's and don'ts, but it is allowing God to be original in our lives. As we are sensitive to the leading of the Holy Spirit and follow the direction He gives, God works in and through us. Galatians 3:11 suggests that no one can ever win God's favor by trying to keep the Jewish laws because God has said the only way we can be right in His sight is by faith. The Prophet Habakkuk says that the man who finds life, finds it through trusting God. (*See* Habakkuk 2:4; Hebrews 10:38; Romans 1:17.)

A hymn that is very meaningful to me is "Trust and Obey." The concept of obedience is expressed in a beautiful way:

> When we walk with the Lord
> In the light of His Word,
> What a glory He sheds on our way!
> While we do His good will
> He abides with us still,
> And with all who will trust and obey.

Have you listened to any grandparents recently and seen their excitement as they talk about their grandchildren? Or have you listened to a young man who has just discovered his companion for life? These people can be so full of the joy in their relationships that they couldn't possibly keep still about it.

So our relationship with God can overflow as we share with hearts full of joy, love, and gratitude concerning what God has done for us. Paul says in Colossians 1:28, "So everywhere we go we talk about Christ to all who will listen, warning them and teaching them as well as we know how. We want to be able to present each one to God, perfect because of what Christ has done for each of them" (LB).

We are commanded in the Scriptures to share our faith, and we're promised the power of the Holy Spirit to do it (*see* Acts 1:8). As a new believer, I wanted to tell others about Christ, but I was concerned for fear that I couldn't do it well because I wasn't familiar with Scripture.

Then I read this verse in 1 John 1:3: "Again I say, we are telling you about what we ourselves have actually seen and heard, so that you may share the fellowship and the joys we have with the Father and with Jesus Christ his Son" (LB). From that verse, I realized all I had to do was share what I had "seen and heard"—what God had revealed to me at that point in my life. As I did, I found many people were looking for the answers I had found. Even though I didn't know a lot about the Scriptures, people were interested in what had happened to me.

From hundreds of thousands of surveys taken by the Campus Crusade staff, we have learned that an average of one out of four people in this country who are not Christians and hear a clear presentation of the Gospel from an individual who is controlled by the Holy Spirit will receive Christ. In some areas of the world the response is one out of two. In much of Africa, nine out of ten receive Christ after hearing the Gospel as contained in the *Four Spiritual Laws*. There's no thrill quite so great as seeing someone else come to trust Christ because you have been faithful and shared your faith.

When I am alone with a person for more than five minutes, I have made it my practice to pursue a conversation with regard to that person's spiritual interests. I try to identify with her in some way that would give us common ground on which to converse. In some situations I only have time to present the *Four Spiritual Laws* booklet and share that these truths helped change my life, and that I think perhaps she personally would be interested. Sometimes I begin by asking, "Have you seen this little booklet?"

One of the most unique experiences I had in sharing my faith was with a girl enroute to Omaha, Nebraska. I was flying from New Orleans to Minneapolis. It had been a long, eight-hour flight with three stops. I had already had two seat partners with whom I had shared and both were extremely interested, though neither had prayed to receive Christ. After the second woman got off, I was ready to rest. However, I prayed that if God wanted me to share my faith again, He would bring along the person who would be the most interested.

Just before the plane was ready to take off, a cute blonde girl dressed in very feminine attire plopped in the seat next to mine. In an irritated voice, she said, "Well, if this plane gets off the ground it will be a miracle." She told me this was the third plane she had boarded to go to Nebraska because there had been mechanical difficulty with each of the other planes.

Matching her mood, I found myself responding, "Well, I

have something for you that will show you why God has put you on this plane." I was amazed that the words came out in such a manner, but I handed this girl a letter my husband had written to a businessman, called the Van Dusen letter, which is an elaboration of the *Four Spiritual Laws*.

After reading a few sentences, she asked sharply, "Where did you get this?"

Briefly I explained.

"Why did you share this with me?"

I told her I had prayed about the person who would sit beside me, and that I had planned to share the letter with that person. As she read more, she often stopped to make comments such as, "This is fantastic"—"I can't believe you'd give this to me"—"This answers my questions"—"I always wanted to know about this."

After finishing she quietly said, "God did put me here beside you on this plane." She explained that she had gone to a very fashionable girls' school and had degenerated morally. She told me there wasn't anything she hadn't done. Several times she had been engaged to be married, only to have the engagements broken. Now there was another man in her life. She said, "If this doesn't work out, I have absolutely nothing to live for." But that day as we talked, she asked Christ into her life.

I received letters from her for several months after our encounter on the plane. She said she had shared the booklet with her boyfriend, and he had prayed to receive Christ. He then suggested she share it with his mother, whom they found was a Christian and had been praying for them. The last I heard, they were planning to establish a Christian home.

As we yield ourselves to the Holy Spirit and share our faith, it's amazing to see the ways God gives us the ability to identify with the person with whom we're sharing. One of the most challenging and exciting times I've had while sharing took place at Arrowhead Springs during a Lay Institute for Evangelism. I was teaching a class on how to use the *Four Spiritual Laws* booklet through a practice demonstration. To help me illustrate, I asked a person from the class whom I wasn't sure was a Christian to sit next to me and role play with me. She was a lovely, sophisticated woman named Christine.

As we were demonstrating the booklet, I mentioned, for the sake of illustration, that she was to respond as a person who did not know Christ, which in no way put her in an embarrassing position.

As we proceeded toward the end of the demonstration, we came to the portion concerning the circle on the left, representing the person who has not received Jesus Christ, and the circle on the right, representing the person who has received Jesus Christ. I simply asked, "Which circle represents your life?" For the sake of illustration she indicated the left circle. Then I asked, "Which circle, Chris, would you like to represent your life?"

She turned to me and said, "Vonette, you aren't going to lead me to Christ. I can't believe all this stuff. The most qualified Christians have tried to explain it, and it just won't work for me." She was not angry or offended; she just didn't want me to waste my time.

God gave me wisdom and I explained that receiving God's gift, Jesus Christ, wasn't the dramatic, emotional experience she believed it to be.

I was sitting next to a coffee table, and while talking I picked up a beautiful ivory inlaid box, which was the only item I'd brought back from Egypt on our trip to the Holy Land. I treasured the artistic box but felt impressed to give it to her to illustrate the point of God's gift to us. So I asked her to receive the box as a gift. She asked whether I was illustrating a point or if I was really serious, and I told her it was for both reasons.

After moments of hesitation, she reluctantly said, "Yes, Vonette, I'll accept the box." As she took it, I explained that receiving Christ was that simple, too.

Then I said, "Chris, will you receive God's gift to you, Jesus Christ, in this same way?" Her eyes became moist and again I asked her if she would like to pray and receive Christ. As we completed the demonstration, Christine prayed that Jesus would come into her heart.

Afterward, as we were talking about how she could be sure Christ was in her life, I told her that as she used the box it would mean she accepted it as her own, and as she trusted God more that would indicate that she had really received His gift, Jesus Christ. I asked her to tell me within the next twenty-four hours if God had become a reality to her.

The next morning, as Bill and I were coming into the dining room at Arrowhead Springs where we were meeting for breakfast, we met Chris and her husband, who were coming down the steps. She ran to put her arms around me and said, "Vonette, I'm using my box." I knew that was her way of telling me Christ was real in her life. Chris and her husband are now being used in a marvelous and fruitful way in Lay Witness Missions in several states.

We're not to be discouraged if we share our faith and the person does not respond. Only God can bring results. "No man can come to me, except the Father which hath sent me draw him" (John 6:44).

Not everyone with whom I share responds. For instance, many people are not ready to make an intelligent decision for Christ, or they may be involved in a moral problem which makes a decision for Christ difficult to make. I have learned that whatever reasons may prevent a person from responding, my responsibility is clear: I simply must share Christ in the power of the Holy Spirit and leave the results to God.

As you actively seek to develop a close personal relationship with Jesus Christ, undoubtedly you will spend time sharing your faith with others, studying the Bible and praying. From the moment you begin, the question "Who is God?" will be central to your life, and the conclusion you reach will affect every aspect of your being.

# 10  Answering the Question

"Who is God?" could be the most important question facing us today, for our view of God determines every facet of our lives. Our answer to this question affects our personal conduct, the way in which we handle our business, the church we choose, the type of educational system we promote, and the kind of government under which we live.

"Who is God?" is such as important question that millions have risked their lives and fortunes seeking an answer. Among these people were the early citizens of the United States. It is obvious from reading the first major documents of our country— the Mayflower Compact, the Declaration of Independence, the Constitution, the Bill of Rights—that our founding fathers believed God to be the Creator of the universe. They were convinced that He was interested in them personally and that He had guided them to this land.

The Pilgrims believed they were commissioned of God to establish a self-governing colony, and so they left England, and then Holland, in search of religious freedom so that they could investigate more deeply the question "Who is God?" The first thing they did after landing in Plymouth was to kneel in prayer, expressing their gratitude for God's direction. They committed their lives to His service and dedicated the establishment of their colony to the glory of God. They also asked for His direction and protection as they boldly started life in their new homeland.

As time passed, the question "Who is God?" continued to determine the actions of America's leaders. During a meeting of the Philadelphia Constitutional Convention, the representatives, in an effort to unite the colonies, came to an impasse. In his book *In God We Trust* Norman Cousins writes that Benjamin Franklin stood and said:

> We indeed seem to feel our own want of political wisdom, since we have been running about in search of it. . . . I have lived, Sir, a long time, and the longer I live, the more convincing proofs I see of this truth—that God governs in the affairs of men. And if a sparrow cannot fall to the ground without his notice, is it probable that an empire can rise without his aid? We have been assured, Sir, in the sacred writings, that "except the Lord building the House they labor in vain that build it." . . . I therefore beg leave to move—that henceforth prayers imploring the assistance of Heaven, and its blessings on our deliberations be held in this Assembly every morning before we proceed to business. . . .

History records that they adjourned and prayed, and when they reconvened, the barriers were removed and our republic's Constitution was soon born. God was very real and important to these men, and they gave Him a vital, priority position in their lives and affairs.

In the early days of the Industrial Revolution, Alexis de Tocqueville, the French historian and writer, came to America to discover the secret of our country's success. He said:

I sought for the secret and genius and power of America in her commodious harbors and her ample rivers, and it was not there; in the fertile fields and boundless prairies, and it was not there; in her rich mines and her vast world commerce, and it was not there. Not until I went into the churches of America, and heard her pulpits aflame with righteousness, did I understand the secret of her genius and power. America is great because America is good, and if America ever ceases to be good, America will cease to be great!

The interest of many Americans in answering the question "Who is God?" has changed from that held by the founding fathers. This lag in interest has brought a moral upheaval unparalleled in this country's history.

It is interesting to note that women have traditionally taken the lead in bringing about a moral change. And never has there been as great an opportunity to effect a positive moral change as there is today. Yet if women are trapped in boredom and are unfulfilled, they will be ineffective in bringing about any change in our nation.

We must recognize that individual women have a choice concerning their responses. Two women's circumstances can be exactly the same. One woman will see God at work in those circumstances, while the other complains, rebels, or resigns herself to a life of mediocrity and lack of fulfillment. The choice is the woman's.

Whichever way we are accustomed to handling the difficulties, God's direction is specific. Reaching our full potential and making our lives really count can begin only when we understand and are rightly related to God through Jesus Christ. He has given us the opportunity to be people guided by Himself—full of His wisdom and power. And as we depend upon Him, we know this promise will be true for us: "Therefore if any man is in Christ, he is a new creature; the old things passed away; behold, new things have come" (2 Corinthians 5:17).

I am only one person, but as I have determined to apply scriptural principles to my life and have shared my knowledge with others, my life has multiplied into many. You are only one, but as you make the same decision, and as other women make that decision, and in turn affect others, it is possible for Christian women to make an impact upon the moral condition of our country and contribute to again making America "good," as de Tocqueville expressed it.

I have desired to make the greatest contribution to society that I possibly can. Often other women ask, "What can I do to also contribute?" or "How can my life really count in changing my community and bringing it back to God?" To help, I encourage Christian women to be involved in at least one secular organization. I do not believe that they should neglect their families or their churches, but that they should simply be available to some organization to contribute where and what they can.

Through the years I have been involved in many different activities, and as a result have met many capable women. I have found that they desire to hear and apply a scriptural viewpoint, but I have also found few women who are able to give it to them. Christian women do not have to run an organization to exert influence. Many times I have been able to share a biblical viewpoint with those in positions to make decisions. Often they have made my words their own and have been far more effective than I could have been.

However, our most important involvement must be within our homes and with our families. We must strive to live consistent, Spirit-controlled, Christian lives and to help our children see the reality of knowing Christ personally. We must also train our children to use scriptural principles in their own lives. To change our communities, we must make sure the members of our own families are being raised according to God's value system.

Another place besides the home where a woman can exert strong influence is in her church. She can encourage activities which will inspire righteous living and not tolerate any actions, conversations, or attitudes that are not glorifying to the Lord.

Only after we have begun with our families and our churches can we look at our community. As we do, an important place to become involved is in the schools. Whether or not we have children in school, we need to be concerned about our educational system. We need to know what is being taught in the classroom and something about the methods being used. We need to be informed about the moral and spiritual values that are being declared, and we must use our influence to see that there be a reinstatement of values based on the Scriptures. For what is taught in the classroom today will be lived in the future.

Christians should also pay attention to the media, for it is one of the strongest influences in our society today. Far too often it is being used destructively. But citizens can exert real influence to help control television and radio programming. The airways belong to the public and the stations' charters are granted for programming that is of interest to the community. If any programming is offensive to you, you can take more action than just turning off the television.

One of the most urgent needs in our nation is to see that men and women of God are elected to public office in our nation, state and local communities. There are many ways to get involved, whether it be through one candidate's organizaton, a party headquarters, or an independent organization.

A woman can also make a significant contribution through prayer. No matter how busy or immobile, she can always pray. She can seek God's viewpoint and think through the issues and then give the direction she is finding to her husband and others who are in positions to make an impact. She can also give prayer support to individuals in positions of leadership, or to those who are ministering to the needs of others.

These are only a few suggestions, but I trust they will help all to think creatively and to contribute in this critical hour.

With all the needs I see in the lives of individuals, as well as in our communities and the nation, I have come to the conclusion that God doesn't give the Christian the alternative of being bored and unfulfilled. A fulfilled life does not come from sitting back and expecting it to come to you. On the contrary, we are to actively pursue it. The person who can apply his faith to significant action is the one who will understand fulfillment.

Through a personal relationship with Jesus Christ, I have personally been able to begin to answer the question "Who is God?" And because of Christ I have had the strength, direction, and courage to try to be the kind of woman who can make a vital contribution. But this response is not only for me to make. It is available to all women today. All we have to do is to decide that we want to apply our faith to become God's maximum women FOR SUCH A TIME AS THIS.

# Appendix

**Managing Yourself**

**Plan Long Range**

    **Pray**

| **Establish Objectives What** | **Program How** | **Schedule When** | **Budget How Much** |
|---|---|---|---|
| **Spiritual** | | | |
| **Mental** | | | |
| **Physical** | | | |

| Establish Objectives<br>What | Program<br>How | Schedule<br>When | Budget<br>How Much |
|---|---|---|---|
| Social | | | |
| Vocational | | | |
| Financial | | | |
| Family | | | |

# Four Spiritual Laws

### LAW ONE

GOD **LOVES** YOU, AND OFFERS A WONDERFUL **PLAN** FOR YOUR LIFE.

### LAW TWO

MAN IS **SINFUL** AND **SEPARATED** FROM GOD. THEREFORE, HE CANNOT KNOW AND EXPERIENCE GOD'S LOVE AND PLAN FOR HIS LIFE.

### LAW THREE

JESUS CHRIST IS GOD'S **ONLY** PROVISION FOR MAN'S SIN. THROUGH HIM YOU CAN KNOW AND EXPERIENCE GOD'S LOVE AND PLAN FOR YOUR LIFE.

### LAW FOUR

WE MUST INDIVIDUALLY **RECEIVE** JESUS CHRIST AS SAVIOR AND LORD; THEN WE CAN KNOW AND EXPERIENCE GOD'S LOVE AND PLAN FOR OUR LIVES.